All-Age
Everything
Revised

Worship for an
intergenerational church

Nick Harding

Augsburg Books
MINNEAPOLIS

ALL-AGE EVERYTHING
Worship for an intergenerational church

© Copyright 2001, 2009 Nick Harding
Original edition published in English under the title ALL-AGE EVERYTHING
by Kevin Mayhew Ltd, Buxhall, England.

Cover image: © iStock 2020: Hand of a child and an elderly person stock
photo by evgenyatamanenko
Cover design: Emily Drake

Print ISBN: 978-1-5064-5984-4

Contents

For all the churches
that have allowed me to practise on them!

Acknowledgements

Thanks to my family, colleagues and supporters who have been there for me during the process of revising this book.

About the author

Nick works for the Church of England in Nottinghamshire encouraging churches to work well and safely with children. He is involved in all-age worship at large events including Spring Harvest and has written children's songs, books for teenagers, Bible notes, and a range of church resources. Nick is a Trustee of Scripture Union and Godly Play UK and is on the C. of E. General Synod. He enjoys travelling on buses, hates sitting still, and delights in his teenage sons and wonderfully tolerant wife!

Introduction

In a number of my previous books and resources I made passing references to the problems and struggles involved in all-age worship, and what it means to be an all-age church. This revised edition of *All-Age Everything* is full of ideas and suggestions to make all-age worship a true intergenerational worship experience.

The separatism of age groups in congregations is, in my view, something to be regretted. We should be looking at ways and places where we can all join together and share. Worship should surely be one of them.

There are many differing opinions on children and their ability to worship. Some churches aim for frequent all-age services as their way of encouraging children to encounter God, while others have given up and rely solely on the groups that the children are sent to during the service. Like all areas of ministry with children, all-age worship is not easy. There are barriers to face, mistakes to make and lessons to learn. But if just one child or adult learns how to worship God in an all-age setting then it will be worth the effort.

Please enjoy reading this and give some of the suggestions a go, but do remember that not every suggestion will be ideal for your church setting. Most of all, remember that meeting God should be fun for the whole church family, however young or old they are.

How to use this book

This is not necessarily a book to read from start to finish, although it may be helpful to do so at least once. As well as being a theory text, it is a resource to be dipped in to, depending on what you are thinking about or what you would like to try. It's your book – do what you like with it!

Theory

The book begins with three chapters on the theory behind all-age worship, how to deliver it well and what formats and orders of service can work well.

Each resource chapter covers a specific area of all-age worship, and looks at some of the theory that underpins it.

Practical

After the theory section in the resource chapters there are many ideas and resources for you to use in all-age worship. These include many prayers, talks, illustrations, suggestions and approaches.

Resources

The book finishes with a section giving names of books, resources and agencies who may be able to help you with your all-age worship.

ONE

For and against all-age worship

I am saddened by the many people who say to me, 'We don't do all-age worship at our church – it doesn't work!' One of the reasons it doesn't work is that there are not leaders who are committed to working hard to get it right. That may mean fighting the corner for all-age, coaxing those who are reluctant to disturb their traditional understanding of worship, and being willing to give adequate time for preparation and planning.

In the Bible, all-age worship worked. Families worshipped together, communities prayed together, and whole nations danced together in praise of God. When Miriam led all the people of Israel in a dance and song of celebration after they had escaped from Egypt over the Red Sea, children mixed with adults as they all celebrated the love and power of God. Modern Jews look on the way the Christian Church treats children with a mixture of sadness and mystification. If all-age worship worked centuries and millennia ago there is no excuse for us not giving it a shot now!

All-Age Everything is based on the following key premises:

1. All-age worship is possible, desirable, and can be excellent.
2. All-age worship is demanding, challenging, and difficult to deliver.

Many churches struggle with what are known as family or all-age services. It seems that in many cases the need to please one sector of the congregation necessarily alienates and upsets the other. Some churches have shied away from them completely, apparently accepting that God's family cannot worship together. Some churches give children things to amuse themselves with, such as crayons and colouring sheets, allowing them to ignore the worship that is going on around them. Others provide a children's service that teaches the adults nothing and makes older members of the congregation feel alienated. Others still aim to make part of the service accessible to children, and then dismiss them from the church so that the 'real' worship can take place. I accept that it can be difficult, and there are a multitude of special challenges involved in providing good all-age services. I know from experience of taking hundreds over the years that they demand more in preparation and thought than the average adult service. Inevitably a busy minister or vicar will want to go for the easier option, and that is to forget about all-age altogether. A question here might be whether church leaders are the ones with the right gifts for this anyway – many lay people are much more skilled in this (and other) areas of ministry. Old and young, parents and children are all called to worship, and worship together. There are times when children and adults need to learn separately, although it is worth saying that at such times the children and young people deserve the best provision possible. There are also times when, for the future of the whole church, children and adults must worship and learn together. I believe it can be and should be done – God's family in a church should be enabled to learn and worship together.

For

Here are a few reasons why all-age worship is important:

1. *Bringing the whole family of the church together: '. . . from whom his whole family on heaven and earth derives its name.' (Ephesians 3:15)*
   Just like in our own families, we may struggle with some individuals. There are people in most churches who don't feel comfortable having children in the church with them, and children who feel alienated by 'disapproving' older folk. But we all gain from being stretched and having to learn to tolerate and grow with things we start off disliking. This model of intergenerational unity gives a powerful example to society.

2. *Providing a family atmosphere and sense of belonging for those who are not part of a traditional family unit.*
If we are not careful this can be seen as being about as subtle as killing an ant with a house brick! We are not trying to patronise those who describe themselves as being single, but we are trying to make them and everyone else feel as if they all belong to the church unit. The family of the church should be seen and felt as being bigger than a collection of family units.

3. *Helping adults look at issues in a simplified, uncluttered way that often gets lost within the complexities of the adult world.*
Theologians know all about the Bible, but they don't all have a living faith in God. The essence of the Gospel is simple and clear, and there's no harm in seeing it that way once in a while. Those adults who say things like, 'That was nice for the children' at the end of a service should be challenged to say what they learned!

4. *Providing children with an opportunity for ministry and a sense of belonging, rather than being shut away somewhere else.*
Some churches have tried sending the adults out of church to small groups and leaving the children in the main church building. This is rarely a popular move, but it does help adults feel the sense of rejection and lack of value which children can feel if sent out of church every week. The main church is usually the most comfortable and expensively furnished space – why should children be excluded from it?

5. *Providing a 'bridge' for unchurched families with a simple but not simplistic service as an introduction to faith.*
We live in a society where unchurched adults have little or no memory of church. In our less literate communities, visitors may find that coping with lots of books and bits of paper and long liturgy is from another culture completely. A more relaxed and less structured service can give them a comfortable place to start to learn and understand. It is an exciting and challenging fact that in many churches the all-age service is the best-attended service of the month. But with this comes a huge challenge regarding the quality and depth of teaching if this is many people's only worship and learning time each month.

6. *Providing suitable teaching for parents to fulfil their responsibility for the spiritual development of their own children: '. . . train a child in the way he should go.' (Proverbs 22:6)*
Let's be clear – it is parents' responsibility to bring their child up as someone who knows about the Christian faith, and they should be willing to sit with them and help them worship during services. But the church can assist this by providing a programme of teaching and services to aid parents in this respect.

7. *Giving those children's workers who look after groups regularly a chance to worship with the church family.*
This is essential in order for children's workers to feel that their ministry is of value. They need to be given time to worship with everyone else so that they can recharge their energy and spiritual awareness. But this should not be an excuse for a morning off!

8. *Providing an opportunity for the church and leaders to worship with, and learn from, the younger church members.*
Children can teach us so much about worship. If we never see the children who are part of our church we never get the opportunity to see God from their point of view, and we miss out. We have so much to learn from children, if only we are willing to do so.

9. *Giving a lesson in tolerance by providing an opportunity for bridges to be built between generations.*
I have often found that those at the top end of the age profile can be much more tolerant of children than those a little younger. Many children likewise have a suspicion about older people, particularly if they have no older relatives. Whatever the situation, it is good for all ages to be challenged and stretched in their acceptance of others.

10. *Provide young people with an opportunity to minister.*
All-age services are ideal opportunities for children themselves to take part. They could lead the service, speak, teach a song, do the readings, or lead prayers. They could be included in the planning, or play in a music group. They should not be dragged to the front to sing a little song, as the focus should be on worship and not patronising performance! Many adults are pleasantly surprised when they see children leading and speaking with wisdom and spiritual insight.

Against

There are many problems with all-age worship, and many people would wish to find critical justification to stop all ages in a church worshipping together. Here are some of the criticisms most commonly put forward:

1. *All-age worship is too hard to prepare.*

   It does take time, prayer, thought and a real commitment to prepare in order to succeed. I don't see how church leaders can justify spending days working on adult sermons and yet not be able to find time to prepare an appropriate service for all ages or help direct a team of others to do so. After all, the whole church deserves leadership and time, not just the adults.

2. *All-age worship tends towards a shallow depth of teaching.*

   'Shallow' and 'simple' are not the same thing! A simple message can help everyone. Most churches only have all-age services every few weeks, and therefore the adults are not going to suffer too much without their weekly dose of theology. Deep theology does not make a good Christian, but a willingness to listen to God does. All all-age services need to focus on one message which is interpreted and made appropriate to all the age groups represented – it can be done!

3. *All-age worship revolves around silly songs.*

   This is nonsense. It does not take noisy, clappy songs alone in order for children to worship. While it is important to make sure that words are appropriate it is also possible to include songs to which adults can relate. Again, simplicity in worship can be a great help or even a liberation for many adults.

4. *All-age services are too active.*

   Since when did worship become a passive spectator activity? Worship is about taking part, demonstrating our love for God, and using our whole being to tell him how much we love him. We should expect to be active and rejoice that God makes it possible to express our worship in so many ways. And even if we are not comfortable with the way some people worship, we have no right to criticise or say that it is in some way inferior.

5. *All-age services tend to be too long.*

   This one is a fair criticism of many services in many churches. Children (and us adults if we are honest) can't take too much in at one time. There is much to be gained by making all-age services shorter than other services – the short, snappy ones are often those that are best remembered. A little time at the end provides more opportunities for people to mix and communicate.

6. *All-age services are not suitable for anyone.*

   All-age services are really difficult to get right. They need to be prepared and led by people who have appropriate gifts, the aim being not to do a 'children's service' but to give children and adults a positive image of God's church meeting together. In some cases it may mean that the church leader or those who usually lead services have to accept that their gifts are not suited to leading all-age, and then invite others with suitable gifts to do them instead. Those adults who absent themselves from all-age worship are depriving the worshipping community of the nourishment that all-age gives. To do an all-age service that meets the needs of the majority takes care, balance and a great deal of prayer. It really does need to be good.

7. *Children do not behave during all-age services.*

   Most children who come to church for all-age services attend with at least one parent. It is the parental responsibility to look after the children and direct their attention to the worship. As the father of two boys I know this is a challenge! On the other hand, the church is guilty of expecting children to behave in a non-child way, and that's got to be wrong too. Boys are made to fidget and have short attention spans – it is in their make up – and to tell them to 'behave' as adults in church is to tell them not to be natural. The bottom line is that the leader of all-age worship should not be expected to 'entertain' the children or discipline them from the front . . . they have got enough to do without that. Ultimately children are more likely to behave if the content of the service is appropriate to them.

TWO

Delivering good all-age worship

Before looking in detail at the ingredients which go into a good all-age service there are a few other issues about presentation and delivery to be considered. Many are very basic, while others are important but often forgotten or ignored. The fact is that in many churches the congregation are more likely to criticise all-age services than other services. These suggestions may help you avoid some of the most common main faults.

Visual aids and gimmicks

'You're the man with a bird in a box,' said a small girl in the queue at a very busy fast-food restaurant where I had gone with my boys. I smiled and said, 'Oh yes, you mean Cheryl the crow,' feeling slightly embarrassed. I continued to chat with the child and her parents, but as the conversation took its course I realised that she had remembered lots about the colour and sound of the puppet, but nothing about what I was trying to communicate through it. That is not necessarily a bad thing, but it reminded me that everything I use should carry a clear message.

Visual aids, tricks and gimmicks do have a part to play in worship. Many of us remember services and talks which had something visual to attract and retain our attention. However, we must be sure that anything we use is visible to the whole congregation, even those at the back or the smallest children. Try kneeling behind a pew or chair to get an idea what children can see. If we have a good idea for a visual aid or something else to get attention we must make sure that it is clearly in line with the theme of the service, not something we are trying to squeeze in for the sake of it. And we should ensure that the visual item does not obscure the message of the service, leaving an abiding memory of something bright or interesting but no idea what it was meant to say about God.

Audibility

I learned an important lesson about audibility many years ago when, at the end of an all-age service in a church I had never visited before, a glowing old lady came to speak to me. She was the sort of person who shone her faith, and I expected a positive and encouraging comment. This is what she said: 'Thank you, young man. It looked very good, but unfortunately I couldn't hear a word. Try slowing down a little, and remember those of us whose faculties are not as young as yours.' I felt admonished and encouraged in one – and I knew she was right.

It goes without saying that everyone in the congregation needs to hear what is going on. If you are to get young people involved in the service they need to be loud, their speech needs to be paced, and they need training and practice in how to use the PA system properly. Even if you are leading a service on your own and have a loud voice, many churches now insist on use of the PA for those with loop settings on hearing aids. Different sectors of the congregation will turn off or glaze over if the service is either too loud or too quiet, if the PA speakers squeal, or if the leader seems to be beaten by the vagaries of wiring.

Children and young people

Any children and young people used in the service should participate with integrity, and not as token gestures or as performing monkeys. Dragging on the Sunday School to sing a twee song during a service should have died out many years ago, but sadly still survives. It may look pretty, it may encourage fringe people such as the children's parents or other relatives to attend, it may even be delightful and inspire an 'Ahhhh' from the congregation, but it is not worship. It is patronising to the children concerned to be used in such a way. It fails adults who should be worshipping with the children, not gawping at them as spectators. If children and young people are involved in the service they should be treated with due respect, and seen as valid contributors. After all, we don't ask adults to show what they have learned during the service and then patronise them with a round of applause!

Length

This is a real problem. Some churches see all-age services as an opportunity to strip the service of anything not deemed to be essential, and consequently go for a minimalist approach that lacks depth. Others try to include everything that every other service has as well as adding in more songs, talks and visuals. As with most things, somewhere in the middle is an ideal service and perfect length.

An all-age service needs to follow a pattern, even if there is a great deal of flexibility within it. The service needs to be long enough to include key elements, while being short enough to keep all ages actively and attentively participating. Some adults may feel short-changed if it is too short, while younger people may feel bored and alienated if it is too long. All churches have their own ideas, but I would suggest that 45 minutes is ample for most all-age services.

Theme and message

I have taken to writing the theme of a service on a large sheet of paper, and placing it on the wall in front of my desk when I am planning. From time to time I look at the theme and think through whether every element of the service fits, and occasionally I get it right!

The theme and message need to be clear, both in the planning and the delivery of a service. It is easy to get bogged down with a great visual or practical idea and lose sight of the original message being given. The theme should be evident in the songs, liturgy, prayers, readings and talk, and the service should aim at leaving worshippers of all ages with one clear and well-defined key message, not lots of disparate ideas. They will not necessarily see all the links straight away, but you will have at least given them a few pointers.

Language

It is of little use leading all-age services with a multitude of long, 'religious' words, or by using language which brings everything down to what we think is the right level for a five year old. It is very easy to patronise the entire congregation by talking down to some for the benefit of others. Great care needs to be given to avoid out-of-date words and catchphrases, while keeping the language relevant and appropriate. This takes plenty of practice, and inevitably leads to mistakes and misunderstandings. But a new look at language can be refreshing and revitalising.

Mixing

I once went to a church where the 'young' (anyone under 40) sat on the left, and everyone else sat on the right. After trying a few jokes and activities to crack the ice, it became apparent that there was something political going on. This church was not one but two. Two clear factions, each of whom viewed the other with mistrust and dislike, had been formed due to disagreements over styles of worship. Now the two sides avoided any sense of worshipping together with any depth.

The congregation needs to mix physically at some point during the service, whether it be to greet each other, discuss things, or pray in small groups. Some traditions have a time called 'sharing the peace' and do move around, shaking hands or (heaven forbid!) hugging. But there are still others who fail to show any form of togetherness and unity and struggle to leave their seats, let alone actually smile. I think it is fair to encourage all the members of the congregation to greet others and work together during services, breaking down the barriers of age and tradition. No particular age group finds this easy to begin with, but all benefit in the long run.

Variety

You may have noticed how short individual scenes on TV are. We are used to fast-moving images and information being given to us in a wide range of ways.

All services need a touch of variety; all-age services particularly so. You should be looking to have a range of voices involved so that the whole service does not fall on to one person. There should be different things happening, loud and quiet, participatory and passive activities, things to look at and things to do. Through a range of voices and styles in the one service many needs will be met and the varied ways people learn best will be attended to.

Accessibility

I visited a church recently on a Sunday when I was not preaching. On the way in I was handed two books and three other pieces of paper. Fortunately I knew my way around the paperwork, but as an 'unchurched' visitor I would have been lost and embarrassed.

If all-age services are used as a 'bridge' for people on the fringe or outside the church, or are going to be attractive to young people, they need to be as accessible as possible. This has implications on the amount of paper worshippers are given as they arrive, the welcome they receive, and the whole atmosphere created by the leader. A special effort needs to be made to ensure that no knowledge or understanding is assumed, while also avoiding boring regular worshippers. We must keep asking ourselves, 'How accessible is this for strangers?'

Directions

It is very easy to make too many assumptions about where the congregation should look or what they should read when leading a service. We may know very well what page to look at for a prayer, that the congregation only read out the passages in bold, or that hymn 237 is in the red hymn book and not the yellow, blue, or green books also in the pews. The problem comes when we are trying so hard to keep an element of pace and movement in the service that we forget to explain the basics or allow time for others to catch up with our thinking. What to us may seem like spoon-feeding will be to others a support and comfort, and help the younger members of the congregation keep up.

Introductions

It never ceases to surprise me how few of the members of my own congregation I know. My excuse is that I am often in other churches on Sundays, and when I am 'playing at home' I am usually leading or preaching. I have had to learn to introduce myself for the benefit of those who haven't the faintest idea who this little man is! Children and adults alike will feel more comfortable if they know who is leading them, who is saying the prayers, and who is preaching. A short one-line introduction suffices, and puts everyone at ease.

Reading the congregation

All who speak to groups should learn to 'read' the audience or congregation. This is particularly important when working with children. It involves watching how they respond to comments and jokes, seeing if they are fidgeting and getting restless, and observing how many have fallen asleep! Expressions on faces and body language are important, and as you lead an all-age service you need to keep an eye on all ages and respond to their unspoken messages accordingly. In simple terms if you sense that things are going well milk it, and if things are going badly head for the home straight!

The children

It may be relevant to bring the children to sit near or at the front for some or all of the service. If you do that remember that you will need other adults to sit with them too, as you cannot lead the service, keep an eye on the congregation as a whole, and discipline the children at the same time. Also bear in mind the importance of families worshipping *together*, not just in the same building. How about suggesting that whole families come to the front and sit on the floor together? If younger children and toddlers are encouraged to be in the service it may be helpful to have a supply of quiet toys available in a particular area for some of the service and draw them in to activities as appropriate, again with adequate supervision.

Children in or out?

I once went to a church to speak at what was called a Family Service. I therefore expected the children to be part of the service all the way through, and for families as well as groups of children to sit together. I was therefore somewhat surprised to see that after 20 minutes all but the oldest children in the 10 plus age group got up and left. Not only did this instil panic into my mind as to what I was going to say to this very altered congregation, it also made me feel angry. Even in a service that was 'marketed' for everyone children were being excluded.

As far as I can see the whole point of all-age services is to provide an opportunity for everyone, however young or old they may be, to laugh, learn, and worship together. Children of all ages, even the new-born and crèche, should be there to represent the family of God to which we all belong. Anything else is a travesty of all-age, and denies God's creativity in making us an intergenerational community.

Notices

Long notices during all-age services are inappropriate, largely irrelevant, and an assured antidote to worship. Verbal notices are not the sign of an active, busy church but a disorganised one which is not able to do a sheet of notices in time. Many who stand up to give notices are very focused on their own project and the sound of their own voice, but not on the listeners who want to worship! And the points in services often chosen for notices are inappropriate too. The beginning should be for individuals to pray and prepare for worship. The middle should be full of God. The end of the service should be for the congregation to reflect and take on board the theme and message. Now, I accept that this seems a little harsh, but having frequently seen how notices can destroy worship and bore worshippers rigid my appeal would be to find a better way of disseminating information.

Communion

There are many strongly held opinions regarding children and communion and this is not the place to examine them. If your church allows children to receive communion then you will be aware that children should receive clear teaching on what they are doing, and that it adds time to the length of the service. In all cases children should not be excluded from seeing what happens, even if the church decides that children should not receive the elements until a certain age, or after a particular process. I would add that it is hard to speak of all-age worship when a significant number of the congregation are excluded from a section of it that is the most 'special', but that is an issue that every church needs to examine for itself. A real intergenerational church will work for inclusion, not exclusion.

Baptisms and thanksgivings

Many churches like to invite families from outside the church to all-age services, a part of which will be the thanksgiving or baptism of their baby. This is good in principle, as the family will be able to take part in a more relaxed and less structured service. However, the negative of this policy is that if the church is packed full of visitors who do not know how to worship, the content and atmosphere of the service is affected. A visiting group of family and friends sitting near the front of the church can make the service very hard to lead. Without being exclusive we have to accept that there are times when just the family of the church needs to meet and worship together, without the inevitable diversion that a thanksgiving or baptism party brings.

Planning

Have you ever wondered how TV chefs manage to cook such good meals so quickly? It is all about preparation! Their ingredients are all prepared in advance, carefully selected and accurately measured by a team of young researchers. Planning is as much the key to good all-age worship as it is to meals cooked in front of the cameras. Good planning

may include children and young people making suggestions as well as taking part, and musicians and others who have particular gifts approached for their advice. Most of all good planning will consider all of the above, and include all of the following. Read on!

THREE

Plans and formats for worship

If we continue to think of an all-age service as a meal then we need to ensure we get the ingredients right, add them to the mixture in the correct order, and constantly evaluate the recipe. Here are some of the ingredients you may use to make all-age worship, with more details given at the beginning of each resource chapter that follows.

- Welcomes and beginnings
- Songs and hymns
- Confessions
- Prayers
- Bible readings
- Talks and stories
- Blessings and endings

All-age worship and Common Worship

Many denominations of the Christian Church have set service patterns and orders which churches can follow. The Church of England has produced and authorised a collection of services entitled *Common Worship*, and various supporting texts for special occasions, church seasons, and so on. This is groundbreaking material using some of the former services in the *Alternative Service Book 1980*, and the original services of the *Book of Common Prayer* of 1662, along with much new and refreshing liturgy. New child-friendly prayers for the Eucharist are also making their mark.

About all-age services

All-age services remain the 'Achilles heel' of many Anglican and other churches because they are so difficult to do well. All too often services are boycotted by adult members of the congregation who find them childish, or boycotted by families with children who find the services tedious and boring. Adults must accept responsibility for their spiritual development outside the church services. *Common Worship* offers an opportunity for churches to think again about worship, including 'family' and all-age services, offering elements which could get a little closer to the impossible task of pleasing all the people all the time.

Background

Many people struggle with family services, with plenty of 'for and against' arguments. In addition there has been concern about the form and content of all-age services for some time. Often they contain little Bible or liturgy, little depth, and too many gimmicks. The book *Patterns for Worship* was finally produced in 1995 and offers a framework for a Service of the Word. The content of the service, and the framework it offers, is now part of Common Worship and recommended for use in all-age and family services. Uniquely, the Service of the Word consists of notes and suggestions rather than set texts, which can be drawn from throughout the *Common Worship* texts. This makes it harder to plough through services with little or no preparation – work has to be done to put a balanced service together.

The shape

Patterns for Worship offers a clear structure for Services of the Word which is ideal as a basis for all-age services. The four sections are:

- Preparation
- Word
- Prayers
- Ending

Texts

Much of the content of a Service of the Word is flexible, and other texts can be found or created. Authorised texts can be taken from *Common Worship*. To obey the 'letter of the law' in Church of

England and Church in Wales churches these are the specific texts that must be used:

- Confession and absolution – many alternatives

- Creed – many alternatives

- Lord's Prayer – four possible versions

Preparation

The service needs a clear beginning which draws the leader and the people together. This could be a response, a greeting, a scripture passage, an invitation to worship, an opening song, or any combination. They should be active, involving the congregation, and in inclusive language. Sign language or actions may be suitable.

Confession and absolution can be in this section, or in the prayers after the Word if penitence is a natural response. There are many authorised prayers of penitence, including seasonal and themed ones.

Word

The Bible should be treated with reverence but not necessarily solemnity – true reverence comes from giving it full weight of meaning.

The Bible reading needs to be delivered creatively. There could be a number of readers, dramatised readings, musical backing, visuals, and so on. It should always be delivered audibly and with respect.

The Word includes the 'sermon' slot. There should not be a separate children's talk; the main talk should be relevant and accessible to everyone. It can be delivered in short sections, with visual aids, drama, interviews, discussion, activity, songs, background music, or any combination.

Creeds and affirmations

There is a range available, including a 'question and answer' version which is more accessible to children than a page of words. Again, it is worth trying music in the background, saying creeds line by line, reading silently, and so on in order to make it more relevant and creative.

Prayers

There are different options available. The Collect (themed or 'of the day') should be earlier or here. Other prayers can be responsive, visual, physical or processional. There should be some space for silence and reflection. Prayers can be led by an individual, a group of all ages, or said in unison.

There are specific themed and seasonal intercessions available in *Common Worship*.

The Lord's Prayer should always be included. There are now four authorised versions, although the versions in Common Worship are most easily available.

Prayers should include a thanksgiving, which may be musical, responsive or spoken by the leader. This will normally be the climax to the Word and prayer sections.

Endings

As with the beginning, a clear end needs to be in place. Services can end with a dismissal, farewell, valediction, blessing, going out or goodbye. There are many options available, and freedom to create your own. Again, creativity and variety are the keys to getting this right.

Creativity

The basic Service of the Word in *Common Worship* offers a familiar framework for the order of the service, with plenty of options. There is room for creativity and originality within the basic shape of preparation followed by Word, prayers and ending. Children, and many adults too, need to feel comfortable in order to worship, and the pattern provides a degree of familiarity. But within those areas leaders need to think creatively, make use of many of the less familiar authorised texts, and present the Word in visual, dramatic or active ways. Then perhaps all-age will mean just that – a service where all ages worship, learn and grow together.

The framework in *Common Worship* offers a degree of freedom and flexibility which should enable churches that have stuck to the BCP to be more creative and flexible, while bringing churches that have no form or order to their family services back to a degree of structure. In either case the use of *Common Worship* has the potential to improve and refresh all-age worship.

Planning

As we have seen before, planning is the key to any effective all-age service. In other words, it is not possible to wing it and get through unscathed. We all accept that planning honours God and the people we serve, but it is difficult to find the time and inspiration to deliver the best. When planning you will need to think through the individual items listed above. Many churches find that it is helpful to form an all-age worship planning team to come up with ideas, even if they are not suited or willing to deliver them. Try to consider the following questions as you plan your service:

1. Is the theme actually clear in my head, and do I understand how the readings relate to the theme? This needs to have been clarified by the time you sit down to plan, and ideally you will have read the readings and been thinking about the theme for some time before that point.

2. Is there any material available that will help me plan? Very few of us are instantly and constantly creative, and we may find it helpful to get ideas that spark us from materials and books. There is nothing wrong with re-using someone else's idea . . . they probably got it from someone else anyway!

3. Can I actually deliver what I have in mind? All churches have resource limitations either in the building or in the people, and sometimes we can be so ambitious in our ideas that we lose sight of what can actually be attained. Be realistic but not restrictive.

4. Who do I need to help me? Don't be afraid to pick the brains of others or rope in colleagues to take part in the service. It is a sign of confidence and maturity to let others work with you, only us control freaks struggle to let go! Accept and use the gifts that God has given you, and encourage others to use their gifts too.

5. Do I know which point I want to stick in the minds of those who worship? The theme and readings should cover the general topic, but you need to be clear on what the end product will be in the minds of adults and children. What gem of Godly wisdom will they take home?

6. Is there something of value for all ages represented? It is good to be reminded that by 'all-age' we do not mean 'children', we mean everybody. As you look through all the items and activities in the service take time to weigh up the balance between things for the younger and older members of the congregation.

7. Can I involve others in this planning? It is worth forming a group to look in detail at each service, and the overall aims of the all-age services. This group should represent the whole congregation, including younger and older people, as all have valuable things to contribute. This may inspire other groups within the church to think about all ages too!

Order of Service

Basic Service of the Word

- Preparation

- Song

- Word

- Prayers

- Song

- Ending

Short all-age worship

- Welcome

- Song

- Confession

- Reading

- Song

- Story / talk

- Prayers

- Song

- Blessing

Full-length all-age worship

- Welcome and beginning

- Song

- Prayers, including confession

- Songs

- Reading

- Visual

- Thanksgiving and offering

- Songs – quiet

- Story

- Talk

- Reflective prayer

- Intercessions

- Song
- Take-away
- Blessing/prayer

All-age worship with baptism or child blessing

- Welcome and beginning
- Songs
- Reading
- Visual
- Thanksgiving and offering
- Songs – quiet
- Story
- Talk
- Reflective prayer
- Baptism/child blessing
- Confession and prayers
- Song
- Take-away
- Blessing/prayer

FOUR

Welcomes and beginnings

Have a think about the beginnings of services in your church. Are they clear? Is there are marked beginning to the time of worship? It is very easy to slide into a service, perhaps cluttering up the beginning with PA problems or notices. It seems obvious that if a service is to have meaning and worth then the beginning needs to be clear and marked. This can be done creatively and imaginatively, or it could simply be a time of quiet and reflection. Whatever you do, try to change it from time to time so that the congregation do not get too familiar with things. Varied beginnings will mark the start of the service better than the same old thing every time.

A few basic questions should help you plan the beginning of the service:

- Is it obvious that the service has begun?

- Are people made to understand that it is worth arriving on time?

- Does the beginning set the tone for the service?

- Is there anything that can help people feel God with them right from the start?

Greeting the congregation individually

Before the service begins, and assuming that everything is tested and ready, it may be worth you breaking down barriers by moving among the congregation and greeting them individually, especially making sure that the children and young people are spoken to as equals to the adults. Then when you get to the front and begin it is more likely that the congregation will be with you.

Begin on time

Make sure that the service begins promptly! I know that in many churches half of the congregation has not arrived by the official start, but the more you let the start slip the less likely it is they will make the effort to get there on time. Visitors will be confused and frustrated by services that seem to begin any time rather than on time.

Carrying or lighting a candle

Many churches find that this simple act brings a sense of peace and the presence of Jesus to what can be a very busy time in the church day. As a candle is carried forward, or someone from the congregation is invited up to light it, the symbolism of the light of Christ can be very effective.

Candle responses

We welcome Jesus,
the light of the world.

As the candle shines,
so your light shines for us.

Jesus is the light of the world,
let us welcome him now.

Light of Christ, shine into me.
Shine into the dark places of hurt and pain.
Shine into the dark places of sadness and regret.
Light of Christ, shine into me.

Jesus, light of the world,
shine in our hearts and lives.

Jesus, the light,
bring light to our worship.

As we light the candle today,
light a flame in our hearts.

In our dark world,
let Jesus bring light.
In our dark hearts
let Jesus bring light.

Greeting the congregation

A simple 'hello' from the front is a good way to begin. You may want to introduce yourself for those who are visitors or not regular attenders. You may want to explain the books and pieces of paper that everyone has got. But please ... avoid notices!

Greeting each other

As we have seen earlier, this is very helpful in an all-age service. Often the beginning is a good time to turn and greet those around, reinforcing the idea of the whole family of the church gathering to worship. Depending on the church this can be a noisy and chaotic time, but it does mark out the beginning of worship.

Sing a song

It may be appropriate to begin straight away with a worship song or hymn, with little or no introduction. This both sets the scene for worship, and keeps the congregation on their toes with a sense of expectancy.

Playing music

A service can begin dramatically by the playing of a popular song, TV theme tune, or advertisement theme through the PA system, as long as there is a link to the theme of the service as a whole. This draws the attention of the congregation and gives the leader a clear link into the theme from the beginning.

The Bible

Many services begin with a word from scripture. This is often linked with the lectionary readings and theme for the day in some denominations. Other verses may be appropriate too, and even a verse taken from the reading.

Opening Bible passages

Worship the Lord your God, and only serve him.

Matthew 4:10

Happy are those whose greatest desire is to do what God requires.

Matthew 5:6

God blessed the seventh day and set it apart as a special day.

Genesis 2:3

Your constant love is better than life, and so I will praise you.

Psalm 63:3

And all the people held a great celebration!

1 Samuel 11:15

I will sing praises to your name.

Psalm 18:49

Praise be to the name of God forever.

Daniel 2:20

May the peoples praise you, O God, may all the peoples praise you.

Psalm 67:3

All the believers continued together in close fellowship.

Acts 2:44

Prepare in the wilderness a road for the Lord!

Psalm 40:3

They took delight in worshipping the Lord, and he accepted them and gave them peace on every side.

2 Chronicles 15:15

Responsive prayers

The advantage of opening the service with a responsive prayer is that it involves and includes the congregation from the beginning. Always ensure that the prayers with responses are on sheets or a projector and visible to all the congregation, and try to avoid making the prayers too complex.

Opening responsive prayers

In all we do, and think and say
be with us now, our Lord, we pray.
In our worship, thoughts and praise
be with us now, and all our days.

Thank you that you were there in our past.
Thank you, Lord.
Thank you that you will be there in our future.
Thank you, Lord.
Thank you that you are here now.
Thank you, Lord.
Thank you that we are here now.
Thank you, Lord.

The Lord is here.
He is with us.
The Lord is here.
He helps us worship.
The Lord is here.
He helps us learn.

The Lord our God is here.
And we welcome him now.

As we come to worship and praise,
Father God, we welcome you.
As we come together in friendship,
Father God, we welcome you.
As we come to listen and learn,
Father God, we welcome you.
As we bring our worries and problems,
Father God, we welcome you.

Why are we here?
We are here to worship God.
Why are we here?
We are here to hear from God.
Why are we here?
We are here to pray to God.

Lord, we invite you into our church.
Lord, we invite you into our church.
Lord, we invite you into our minds.
Lord, we invite you into our minds.
Lord, we invite you into our hearts.
Lord, we invite you into our hearts.

Come and be with us, Father God.
Be in our worship.
Come and be with me, Father God.
Be in my heart.

Action welcomes

Physical actions and sign language can be very powerful and moving. Many are simple to do with a little imagination, or you may have access to someone with sign-language skills who can help interpret some of these simple statements. Try saying them at the same time, and doing the actions silently. I have found that actions draw a congregation together, and are accessible even to the youngest and oldest of worshippers.

AWE

Try this simple action to be used in worship as an example, and then develop your own. Explain that the word AWE is used to express how incredible and beyond our understanding God is. Then lead the children in raising their hands and pointing up, saying the word Amazing, making a circle shape to illustrate the round world and saying Wonderful, and bringing their hands in front of them and doing a 'thumbs up' saying the word Excellent. Once you have done that do the actions while saying this statement together: 'God, you are amazing, wonderful and excellent.'

We clap our hands to welcome God *(clap hands).*
We move our feet to celebrate *(dance).*
We raise our hands to worship God *(raise hands).*
We shout out our praise *(shout out words of praise).*

We are here to worship *(hands up).*
We are here to pray *(hands together).*
We are here to listen *(hands on ears).*
We are here to praise *(hands move from lips).*
We are here to meet God *(hands shake together).*

Jesus *(finger points to the palm of the other hand).*
Here I am *(point to yourself).*
Rise up to worship *(move from behind pews
    onto feet).*
I welcome you, Jesus *(beckoning movement).*
Please give me your love today *(hands open).*

Opening prayer

There are plenty of examples in approved service orders published by various denominations, and many leaders are capable and confident to prepare their own opening prayers. The key to an opening prayer in an all-age service is that it is short and relevant.

Opening prayer

Father God,
we thank you that you have called us here today.
Help us to be open to all you have to say to us.
Amen.

Dear God,
we are here with our families and friends.
We are here with our neighbours and colleagues.
We are all here to worship you. Help us.
Amen.

Father God,
clear away our worries and concerns.
Take away our unhappy thoughts and memories.
Ease our doubts and sadnesses.
Fill our minds and hearts with love for you.
Amen.

We have gathered here to meet with our God.
We are young and know there is more to learn.
We are old and wish we had learned more.
We pray that our hearts and minds will be open.
We have gathered here to meet with our God.
Amen.

Dear God, move in us through your Spirit.
Speak to your children, young and old.
Make us love you more this morning.
Amen.

God the three in one, fill us with your love.
Help us to worship, fill us with your joy.
Help us to learn, fill us with your understanding.
Amen.

FIVE

Songs and hymns

As adults we take worship for granted and so often go through the motions. Some churches have 'hymn sandwiches', others 'worship song sandwiches'. Once we know the pattern of worship in our church we can easily pretend, and therefore not be touched by God or reach out to him. Yet the reason we worship is to honour God, and through it God wants to meet with us and speak to us. As we sing songs and learn the words, we take on the meanings and theology contained in them, and learn more about God through them. That isn't to say that all hymns and worship songs contain words and sentiments which we personally support or understand. There are phrases such as the classic 'ineffably sublime' which is wonderful language but not so marvellous in terms of communication. There are also plenty of 'Right, Jesus, give me everything you've got NOW! I'm waiting!' songs that strike me as being a little arrogant. Whatever we think of newer or older forms of worship we have to remember that the children in our congregations do enjoy singing and can learn so much about God and about worship through songs.

When planning the songs for an all-age worship service ask yourself these basic questions:

- Is there something for everyone?
- Are the words of both traditional and modern hymns appropriate?
- Is there opportunity for all ages to be involved?
- Are some of the songs patronising or childish?
- Are the songs taught and led well?
- Is the choice made by children and adults?
- Are all ages involved in playing instruments?

There are now a lot more song books which have worship songs suitable for both children and adults. There is a list of many in chapter twelve.

Here are some further thoughts about the songs we choose for our all-age worship:

Aim for a balance

We should not work on the assumption that because children are present all the songs have to be new, easy and lively. In order to provide something for everyone it may be necessary to include hymns that are not very child-friendly but are appreciated by older members of the congregation. One approach is to 'top and tail' the service with traditional hymns, and have more modern songs in the middle of the service.

Don't choose songs which are flippant or pointless

There are plenty of such songs around, and they do nothing to honour God or help children or adults understand more about our faith. If we are trying to teach that worship and praise is about communication with God we demean it by choosing and using songs which are a waste of words and time, and only serve to alienate some sections of the congregation gathered. So much can be learned through the right songs with the right words.

Encourage the learning of words

It is easy to rely on songbooks or projectors but many people find it difficult to read the words, pick out the tune, and think about what they are singing at the same time. It can be very helpful to learn the words of simple songs and explain the more complex concepts and words. In order to avoid confusion and misunderstandings, difficult phrases and words should be explained in straightforward language and words learned line by line if necessary in order to aid the learning, meaning and freedom in worship.

Introduce a range of songs

There are sure to be favourite songs which your church always uses in all-age worship, and which can easily become tried, tested . . . and tired! It is much better to work towards a balance of new songs and old favourites. There are many new worship songs for adults which can be used with children too, and are therefore ideal for all-age worship. There are also many newer songs for children and young people which adults can also enjoy. There are some very good books (*Everybody Praise* from SU, *Kidsource* from Kevin Mayhew Ltd, and the annual *Kids' Praise* books from Spring Harvest/ICC) containing exciting, well-written and meaningful newer songs which go down well with all ages and teach real truths.

Introduce a variety of styles

Ensure that there are fast and slow songs, songs with deep meanings and others with clear and simple messages, and songs which everyone can really enjoy singing. There should be quiet songs, songs with actions and signs, louder and more active songs, and songs which stretch the understanding a little. Some adults may take some encouragement to join in, but can be persuaded by a little gentle, good-natured pressure.

Be lively in worship

Worship and praise when children are present is often only interpreted as being the use of noisy and 'happy clappy' songs. Let's not lose that thought – it is right to sing praise to the Lord, dance, and enjoy being lively in our worship. In Exodus 15 Moses and the people sing in praise of God, followed by Miriam and other women leading a dance with prayers, songs and tambourines. Children are wonderfully uninhibited and free in their celebration of their love for God, and just because children are good at it does not make it a childish thing to do. As adults we have much to learn about free, uninhibited worship, with a desire to celebrate and an awareness of the joy that only God can give. For the whole church family action songs can be great fun, fast songs can give children a glimpse of the joy of knowing God, clapping is great, and it's all thoroughly biblical.

Be quiet in worship

Many adults feel most comfortable when worshipping quietly, and that is a skill which children need to learn too. In a noisy and busy society quiet is refreshing and unusual, but can take some getting used to. As with everything to do with all-age worship, balance is the key. In 1 Kings 19 we see that Elijah was going through a hard time. He was feeling weakened after a spiritual battle, and wanted to hear God and receive refreshment. But God couldn't be found in the noise of the wind, earthquake or fire. He was only found in silence. So it is now – children and adults together can worship quietly if the songs chosen help them move closer to God, and their openness can be a true example to the 'mature' Christians in the pews next to them.

Amazement and delight

Help the congregation to develop that sense of amazement and delight in God. Keep reminding them that the God who created everything cares for them and knows them individually. Allow them to use words in songs that are culturally relevant to them and express how they feel, and make sure that they understand what worship is all about. This is so important, even for the older people who think they know all about God. There is so much more for us all, and it can be found through worship.

Giving singing value

Don't use singing (or prayer for that matter) as a 'time filler', something that must be done out of tradition, or as a stopgap – it's more important than that! The opening song should set the tone for the whole service, and the other songs chosen should have something worthwhile to say. If we place singing in worship low in our list of service-planning priorities we devalue it, and make it seem of little importance or relevance to younger and older people alike.

Freedom while singing

Encourage a freedom in worship, and set an example. Some people, particularly those who are used to traditional church services, may need to be taught and encouraged to let go in all-age worship and enjoy the fun of celebrating the love of God. Much of this relies on your willingness as a leader of all-age services to be seen to enjoy worship yourself, setting an example to your elders, peers and young people. The more we are willing to show ourselves worshipping through songs the more likely it is that the congregation will be willing to follow and learn from us. Worship in our all-age services is for all of us, children, adults and leaders alike.

Actions and stances

Encourage worshipful stances, actions and attitudes. Some people worship well with their eyes closed, hands open or arms raised. Everyone in the congregation should be encouraged to use the stance that suits them and helps them express their adoration and love for God:

- Stand with hands open to receive from God.
- Close eyes while the leader says the words at the start of each line.
- Turn and face a focal point for worship (e.g. a cross, the altar).
- Raise hands.
- Clap along to the music.
- Encourage all ages to use simple percussion instruments or shake keys.
- Kneel in adoration.
- Gently sway to illustrate the movement of the Holy Spirit.
- Use simple actions or sign language.
- Move around in procession while singing.
- Sing lively songs as people leave their pews at the end.

Favourites for all

Have a vote amongst everyone in the congregation as to which songs and hymns are their favourites. Try to include all the songs and hymns chosen in services over the coming months, and if possible ask some of those who have chosen the reasons why it is their favourite. This should include the whole family of the church, and help different generations understand each other a little better.

Actions for all

When using a children's song with familiar actions, miss out the words from time to time and have actions only. This is both good fun, and helps children concentrate on the meaning of the words they are used to singing. Then move on by choosing a song that is familiar to the adults and add simple actions to it. This will reinforce the idea that worship is not just about singing but about our actions too, and that adults can worship through action songs. Again, try not singing but simply doing the actions at least once through. This helps everyone think through the words of the song.

Dance in worship

Work with those adults, teenagers and children who choose to be involved in the preparation of a dance to a quieter or slower worship song which they could also sing while dancing. Offer it as a contribution to whole church during all-age worship as appropriate. This is best done as an all-age activity to avoid criticism that dance and movement in worship is only for children.

All-age orchestra

Encourage children and adults to join in with the music by playing their own instruments if they have any, or by using percussion instruments. This will need some co-ordination, but speaks volumes about how all ages can work and worship together. You could form a permanent group to lead the music in all-age services, hold regular practices, and get others involved by doing a workshop to make basic percussion instruments before they play them.

Confessions

Many church traditions have a time near the beginning of the service to say sorry to God for our failings and sins. There are a number of possible words given for this in service books such as *Common Worship*. But words are only part of the process, and we can breathe new life into this part of the service by thinking of more creative ways to bring our confession to God, and receive his forgiveness. First of all, a few questions:

- Is there a purpose for it, or is it there through tradition?

- Is the confession at an appropriate point in the service?

- Does it make people feel they are always having to say 'sorry' to God?

- Is it a positive, helpful experience for worshippers?

- Is there variety and creativity in the way it is done?

- Are the words used accessible to all ages?

Explain what is happening

If you use the formal words from a service order it is helpful to explain to the congregation and put it in context for all ages. You may want to introduce the confession and forgiveness by using set words of explanation.

Confession introductions

We all go wrong, and say or do things which fail others, and fail God. As we worship God it is good to say sorry to him. So let's be quiet for a moment and think of the things we have said or done which have been wrong during the last few days. Then I shall say some words, and you can join in with the words in dark print. Every one of us has hurt other people, and as we hurt others we hurt God. Every one of us has said and thought wrong things, and as we say and think wrong things we hurt God.

Let's spend a little time saying sorry to God for the hurt we have caused him.

If we say we don't go wrong we deceive ourselves, and we are not telling the truth. If we say sorry to God he promises to hear us, and to forgive us.

Traditional confessions

Following a traditional confession is helpful for many of the older members of the congregation, and can be good for all ages if not so over-used that it becomes familiar and tedious. We do not want children to feel that going to church is only about being sorry to God!

Confessions

God knows what we are like. He knows that there have been times when we have not done or said helpful things, and when we have done or said unhelpful things. He wants us to remember those times and bring them to him as we pray, asking that he will hear us and forgive us.

Father God, we know in our hearts that we have gone wrong, and we know that you understand. Please forgive us, and help us to make a fresh start.

I'm sorry, God, for the times when I have wanted more than I need.
I'm sorry, God, for the times when I have wanted to be in charge.
I'm sorry, God, for the times when I've not thought about others.
I'm sorry, God, for the times when I have thought about me and not about you.
Thank you, God, that you forgive me. Amen.

If I could start again and take back what I said, I would do so.
If I could start again and do what I should have, I would do so.
If I could start again and not do those wrong things, I would do so.
Help me to start again, to change, and to be made new.

Father God, you know how we feel, and we ask you now to forgive us. Help us to begin again, trying hard to do and say only helpful things. Amen.

Lord God, who made us and loves us, we have done wrong. We have said things that were bad, and done things that caused pain. Help us to show our love for you by being really sorry, and trying harder to get things right in the future. Amen.

Play music

Have quiet music, either live or recorded, playing while the words of a traditional confession are said. This can help in bringing a sense of peace and reverence to the moment, and somehow helps bring new meaning to familiar words.

Read it all

Rather than having the congregation join in at the usual points, read the whole passage yourself. Encourage everyone to think carefully about the words you are saying, and allow plenty of time for reflection.

In the bin

Hand out small pieces of paper and pens at the start of the service, and then encourage everyone to write down things they have done that they are sorry for. Remember that younger members of the congregation, and older ones too, may need a little help with this activity. Then as the confession is said have a bin brought through the congregation and invite them to throw their pieces of paper into it. This symbolises God taking away our guilt, and helping us start afresh.

Bring it out

Again, have the congregation write down things they repent, but this time sing an appropriate song while everyone comes to the front and places the paper on a table or the altar. You could then burn the papers (ensuring safety is paramount!), throw them away, or leave them where they were placed.

To each other

Form the congregation into mixed-age groups of families and others. Then ask them in their groups to read the confession and forgiveness to each other. Some may feel comfortable with placing hands on others or joining hands as they pray.

The slate

A good image to explain what confession can mean is to talk of a slate, and how God accepts the things we do that make it dirty, and wipes it clean. It can sometimes help to have a slate and write on it suggestions from the congregation of things we do wrong, and then wipe it clean after prayer.

Move around

Read through the confession as usual, and then invite all members of the congregation to stand and move around, greeting each other and saying words such as:

God forgives you.

God offers you his love and forgiveness.

Receive the forgiveness of God and start afresh.

The slate is wiped clean.

Father God says, 'Begin again.'

In unity God forgives and takes us forward.

Themed confessions

Some of the confessions in new service orders have themes to them. It can be very helpful to have confessions that follow the subject of the service.

Love

You have given us so much love,
but we have not accepted it.
You have shown us how to love,
but we have not learned it.
You have told us who to love,
but we have not done it.
You have told us the cost of love,
but we have not appreciated it.

We are sorry for not understanding your love.
We are sorry for not sharing your love.
We are grateful for the love you offer, even now.

The world

For the times we have been greedy,
forgive us, Lord.
For the pollution we have created,
forgive us, Lord.
For the peoples we have ignored,
forgive us, Lord.
For the world we have damaged,
forgive us, Lord.
For the love we have not given,
forgive us, Lord.

Commitment

In our lives of faith we have let you down
when we have thought bad things about others,
avoided the needy, and failed to help.
In our lives of faith we have let you down
in the way we are at home, the things we do
at school, the actions we take at work.
In our lives of faith we have let you down
when we could have shared about you, or offered
to pray for others, or spoken of our faith.
In our lives of faith we have let you down.

Help us to be committed to you today and every
day, and take every opportunity to serve you.

Lifestyle

There is a way that we should live,
but we like to live other ways.
There is a way that we should live,
where love for others is at the centre.
There is a way that we should live,
where selfishness and greed have no place.
There is a way that we should live,
and that is your way.
There is a way that we should live,
help me to live your way.

The world has changed me, and I am sorry for it.
The world has changed the way I spend my money –
help me to use your generosity wisely.
The world has changed the way I see relationships,
help me to really value those I love.
The world has changed the way I think about things.
Help me to think with your understanding.
The world has changed me, and I am sorry for it.

Remembrance

For the times in the past when mankind killed and
hurt others, and for the times when people have
ignored you:
Father, forgive us and help us.
For the times when we behaved badly towards
others and caused pain, enjoying hatred and ignor-
ing peace:
Father, forgive us and help us.

We remember those who have struggled for us,
we remember those who have suffered for us.
We remember that this isn't part of God's plan.
We remember those who have given for us,
we remember those who have died for us.
We remember that this isn't part of God's plan.

SEVEN

Prayer

Prayer is a vital part of worship and praise. We use prayer to say thank you to God, to express our love and to communicate our desires, as well as for listening and being quiet. Yet often our prayers become a litany of begging and persuading rather than an inspirational and meaningful experience. If we hope that all the people in our churches will develop meaningful personal prayer lives we have to teach them to pray. As we prepare our all-age services and think through elements of prayer, here are a few initial questions:

- Are they fitting prayers for church worship?

- Do they involve the congregation, both adults and children?

- Is the language inclusive of all ages?

- Is the language inclusive of both genders?

- Is prayer integral to the service or 'tacked on'?

- Do the prayers relate to the theme and teaching?

The prayer of praise and thanks which many of us will know as the Magnificat (Luke 1:46–55) is what a prayer in worship should be like. It follows no particular set pattern but reveals a number of different facets of the nature of God. Firstly we see God being personal and intimate, directly involved in the life of the worshipper, in this case Mary. She recognises God's involvement in her life and celebrates the fact that God loves her. Then we see the awesome nature of our creator God, who made all things. He has shown mercy and used his power over generations. Finally we see the faithful nature of God. He has kept his promises over generations and shown mercy to mankind. This is our God, and this is some prayer!

Prayer is something which, in this paradoxical world, young people can grasp easier than ever before. We have technology which enables us to talk to people who are far away while walking along the street and send messages via a computer screen. There is only a very short step to go to the idea of communicating with God through our thoughts and words! The reality of God in their lives which many people in churches take for granted makes them open, freeing them up to be released into active and life-changing prayer which others may think is strange or beyond them. There are many adult church members who need, but can't find, a prayer life as stimulating as that which many children take for granted. In this and other things, adults can learn from the children sitting next to them.

Personal prayer

It is important that there is space in any all-age service for individuals to speak to God. This could be at the beginning of the service, or at the end in order to reflect on what God has been saying. We must also help others feel free to talk to God about anything that is on their minds. Some people in the congregation may feel able to share about their own prayer life as an encouragement to others, and it may be relevant from time to time for a leader to speak about how they structure their own prayer time with God. This is an issue which has no age limitations – personal prayer is vital for all.

Leading prayers

Many of the prayers used in all-age services will be led from the front. There is a vast range of prayers in service and prayer books. While these prayers can be useful, it is still important to remember that the language needs to be relevant, the prayers should not be too long, and they should be linked with the theme of the service.

Responses

Some churches and denominations will be more familiar with responses than others. Responses help participants feel that they 'own' the words that are being said, and they tend to listen better. They help keep the people's minds 'on task' as the leader prays short phrases with simple responses at the end of each. As they get used to the idea of prayers with responses the congregation could be encouraged to say the phrases in-between.

Prayer responses

For . . .
Thank you for everything, Lord.

Dear God, hear our prayer.

For . . . and all our needs.
We bring our needs to you.

We bring our prayers to you,
because we know you answer.

Thank you that you hear.
Thank you that you answer.

Merciful God, who shows us love,
hear our prayers today.

For . . . Father God,
to you we pray.

You are listening,
and you hear our prayers right now.

For all these things,
for all these things we thank you .

Hear what we ask you,
and answer our prayer.

The Lord's Prayer

Most people will know at least one version of the Lord's Prayer as taught by Jesus (Luke 11:1–4) and altered little over the 2000 years since! This prayer has it all, and it is worth taking it apart from time to time and explaining it to children and adults alike. Through the Lord's Prayer we recognise the Lordship of God, we call for his kingdom to grow, we ask for our needs to be met and we seek his forgiveness in a brief confession. After that we ask God to go with us and protect us, and again we pray for his kingdom to be recognised and to grow.

In all-age services it is best to use a modern version of this prayer, and have it available for anyone to read if they need it. Try to say it with meaning, have time to pause during it and think what it means, or there are also a number of versions of the Lord's Prayer set to music. Most of all, do all you can to stop the words of this essential prayer becoming jaded.

The Lord's Prayer

Our Father, you are in heaven
and your name is special and wonderful.
May your plans become reality,
and all you desire happen in our world and
    in yours.
Please give us all we need to get through today.
Forgive us for all we have got wrong,
and help us do the same for those who hurt us.
Keep us from doing things that are wrong,
and protect us from hard times.
Everything in heaven and on earth is made
    by you and belongs to you,
and that's the way it will be . . . always.

General prayers

When things are going really well in the future
I will remember to thank you.
When I am tired or ill in the future
I will ask you to help me.
When I feel sad and hurt in the future
I will ask you to comfort me.
When I am much older in the future
I will remember to thank you. Amen.

Thank you, God, that you give us all we need,
    so there is no need to worry.
Thank you, Jesus, that you called yourself the Good
    Shepherd.
You look after us all, even when we feel . . .
Help us to ask you for help when we are worried
    about things.
Amen.

For a future hope in our world,
for a time when peace will replace war
and love will replace hatred:
Father, be with us and help us.

For a future hope in our church,
for a time of true care and fellowship
and real love for our community:
Father, be with us and help us.

For a future hope in our lives,
when we learn to live your way and bring peace
into our own families and friendships:
Father, be with us and help us.

In thanks we worship you, O God.
In thanks we seek your will, O God.
In thanks we pray for our needs, O God.
In thanks we pray for the needs of others, O God.
In thanks we trust you, O God.

We thank you for the love you have given us,
and we pray that we will share that love.
We thank you for the gifts you have given us,
and we pray that we will use those gifts.
We thank you for the peace you have given us,
and we pray the world would know that peace.

Everybody here was designed by you,
and that's amazing!
Everything we are was planned by you
and that's amazing!
Everything we have was provided by you,
and that's amazing!
Every good hope we have was placed there by you,
and that's amazing!
Everything, everyone, by our creator God,
and that's amazing!

For all our greed, we pray for your forgiveness.
For all our needs, we pray for your provision.
For all our troubles, we pray for your rescue.
For all our hopes, we pray for your direction.
For all and everything, we pray to you.

As we think of the world we think of needy people,
people in pain, poverty and war.
As we think of our community we think of
   needy people,
people in despair, sadness and misery.
As we think of our church we think of
   needy people,
people in sickness, fear and loss.
As we think of you we think of our God,
God who answers all our prayers. Amen.

Others leading prayer

Many people will be willing to write prayers and share them with others in church as part of a service. Families may be willing to do so, but this can appear rather 'cutesy' to those who are in church

but not in that form of traditional family. It may be better to ensure that a group is drawn from all ages. In all cases make sure that those leading prayers are aware that it is an all-age service, know the theme, and understand where to stand. The language used in prayers both with children and adults needs to be 'despiritualised' so that leaders of prayer have the confidence to pray out loud and not feel the pressure of getting the 'language' right.

Free prayer

Different churches have different traditions as well as physical constraints which may make open prayer difficult. However, if it is possible to have short times of open prayer during an all-age service it should be encouraged. Make sure that everyone can hear what is said, that no one is allowed to dominate the time, and that you as the leader are always in control.

Prayer through objects

You may want to encourage the congregation to focus on an object or image during a time of prayer. With their eyes closed or open the congregation can focus on things like a candle, picture or icon. They may need some guidance, such as ideas about what to think about, and the leadership of this should be gentle and sensitive.

Prayer with music

Playing quiet music can be effective in helping all ages settle down to quiet and focus on God. People are generally not used to being quiet and if there are noise disturbances from outside or other rooms, having calming music in the background enables them to listen and think about God.

Intercessions

We should all be reminded from time to time that prayer is not just about us. Looking back again to the Lord's Prayer we see intercession interwoven with prayers of thanks and our own personal needs. As we communicate with God through prayer we must learn to have other people and situations in mind, and bring those to God with a belief that he hears and answers. Every church has people who are in need of prayer, and those people should be prayed for in services when everyone is together. If the church as a whole has decided to financially support a situation, individual or agency they should be encouraged to get into the habit of praying for them. But intercession must not be seen as long, boring 'shopping lists' of things we demand from God ... it is so much better than that!

Prayers from suggestions

It is sometimes good to get the thoughts of the congregation when you come to prayer. They may have particular needs, or want to extend the theme of the service further. You will need a flip chart and pens to do this, and remember that all the suggestions need to be prayed for.

Visual intercessions

It may be possible to have an item which represents each section of the intercessions, and can be used as a visual focal point for those who want to keep their eyes open when praying. Examples could be:

- Globe – the world
- Toy gun – wars and peace
- Bandage – sick and ill
- Bible – evangelism and mission
- Food – famine and suffering
- Church photo – the church and leaders

Orders of intercessions

It is important to make sure that a range of things are prayed for, and that nothing important is missed off. Set intercessions in traditional prayer books usually go through a range of subjects. Here is a suggested order of intercessions and introductory words:

The world

For God's kingdom to come and bring peace to people and places that don't know him. For the world to be loved and protected, not destroyed by humankind.

We pray for this world, made and loved by God ...

The country

For leaders and government to look to God for guidance, and for the country to live with the morality and faith that God has called us to live by.

We pray for this country and all in power ...

Crisis

For areas or people in current special need, for natural and man-made disasters, and people who are in the headlines and in distress.

We pray for all in special need, including ...

Community

For local people, that God would be with them, and that they would see that he is their creator, and he loves them.

We pray for this area, our friends and neighbours ...

Church

For the church, that it would be a light in the darkness of the world around, and that it would be obedient to God and grow stronger.

We pray for this church, the people and the power of God here ...

Individuals

For those who are sick, those bereaved, and others we are able to name who are in special need.

We pray that the power and love of God would be with ...

Ourselves

For God to continue to be with us as we worship during this service and during our lives.

We pray for the people next to us, and for ourselves ...

Encouragement through answered prayer

God tells us that he is like a good parent who only wants to give good things to his children. He promises to meet our needs for food, clothes and other basics, and calls on us to pray for healing and other needs. So we should be expectant people, waiting for God to answer the prayers we give him and willing to share the joy of those answers.

Younger members of the congregation rarely remember what we say to them in the long-term, but they do remember our attitudes and habits. They will remember if we get into the habit of openly sharing when we have experienced God answering our own personal prayers. And for children even the most seemingly trivial answer to prayer has real meaning and significant positive effects. Building in an all-age opportunity to share about answered prayer is valuable in encouraging children and adults to pray more, and in turn in helping the church grow.

Signs and actions

Many people are now becoming skilled in sign language, and it is a very powerful and effective tool in prayer. Simple signs can be tied together to make a visual rather than said or silent prayer. For instance, the response, 'Thank you, God, for loving me' is simple enough for everyone to learn basic actions to, and remember well. The power of physically communicating our love for God should not be underestimated.

Thanksgivings

In prayer we should remember that it is an opportunity to thank God for all we have and for all he is, as well as a time to bring needs to him. Thanksgivings can help us focus on the things in our lives which are precious and meaningful. There are many already available in service and prayer books.

Thanksgivings

Give thanks, give thanks to the God above.
Give thanks to him for ever.
Give thanks, give thanks to the God of love.
Give thanks to him for ever.
Give thanks, give thanks for Jesus the Son.
Give thanks to him for ever.
Give thanks, give thanks for everyone.
Give thanks to him for ever.

As we think of the Son of God, born as a baby,
we bring our offering of thanks to you.
As we think of Jesus, the good man of peace,
we bring our offering of thanks to you.
As we think of the healer, saving and loving,
we bring our offering of thanks to you.
As we think of the Messiah, born to die,
we bring our offering of thanks to you.
As we think of the saviour, dying on the cross,
we bring our offering of thanks to you.
As we think of the risen, alive again,
we bring our offering of thanks to you.
As we think of Christ, living within us,
we bring our offering of thanks to you.

Thank you for the things that make us smile,
thank you for them all.
Thank you for the things that make us feel good,
thank you for them all.
Thank you for the things that refresh us,
thank you for them all.

Thank you for the things that excite us,
thank you for them all.
Thank you for the things that inspire us,
thank you for them all.

We open our eyes and look all around,
made by the Father, thanks be to God.
We open our ears and hear every sound,
made by the Father, thanks be to God.
All that we hear and all that we see,
made by the Father, thanks be to God.
Even my family, my friends, and ME!
made by the Father, thanks be to God.

For the night and the day, the dark and the light,
thank you, thank you, Father God.
For the food we eat, and the things we drink,
thank you, thank you, Father God.
For the homes and families that we come from,
thank you, thank you, Father God.
For the people around us who care about us,
thank you, thank you, Father God.
For the good things of life, for the fun and the joy,
thank you, thank you, Father God.
For everything, for everyone, for everywhere,
thank you, thank you, Father God.

There's a universe you made with stars and planets.
You are the creator, and we are grateful.
There's a world of land and sea and sky.
You are the creator, and we are grateful.
There are animals and birds, pets and people.
You are the creator, and we are grateful.
There are nations and tribes, clans and families.
You are the creator, and we are grateful.
There are people all around, there are young
  and old.
You are the creator, and we are grateful.
There is everything you made, and that
  includes me!
You are the creator, and we are grateful.

Give thanks to God, for he is so good.
His love lasts forever, his love lasts forever.
Give thanks to the greatest of all and everything.
His love lasts forever, his love lasts forever.
Give thanks to the best, the mightiest and
  strongest.
His love lasts forever, his love lasts forever.
Give thanks to the one who can do great miracles.
His love lasts forever, his love lasts forever.
Give thanks to the one who made heavens and oceans.

His love lasts forever, his love lasts forever.
Give thanks to the one who made time and the
    seasons.
His love lasts forever, his love lasts forever.
Give thanks to God, for he is so good.
His love lasts forever, his love lasts forever.

Offerings

Offerings in church worship usually take the form
of a collection of money and then a prayer. This is
fine as far as it goes, but again a little creative thinking
can turn a chore into something fun, memorable,
and meaningful for all ages. For instance, it is
appropriate to talk through with the whole congregation the costs that there are in running a church.
Look at a simplified budget, and ask them to discuss
where all the money comes from. End with a
challenge for them to think through what they can
offer to God.

Creative giving

Try some of the following methods in all-age services
to make the 'offering' more interesting and fun:

Pass around an unusual object to place money in,
such as a hat, a shopping bag, a bucket or a welly!
What it goes in doesn't really matter, but what we
mean as we give does.

Try getting the children to throw their money into a
big box, onto the top of a parachute or play canopy,
or at a target at the front.

Ask a selection of people representing different
generations to come out and pray while the offering
is taken, beginning their prayers with, 'I give to
God because . . .'

Have everyone join with a simple prayer while
they give, repeating it and thinking about the
words as necessary: 'Thank you, Lord, for all we
have. Help us to cheerfully give back to you.'

Offering prayers

There are offering prayers within set services or
other books, said when the collection money is
brought to the front. You can either use one of those
or come up with something original. Here are some
suggestions:

Father God, you have given us so much.
Bless this little that we return to you. Amen.

Dear God, your blessings get better every day.
Help us to bless others through these gifts. Amen.

As we offer our money we say
thank you, Lord.
As we offer you our thoughts we say
thank you, Lord.
As we offer you our lives we say
thank you, Lord.

For fun and games, for friends and family,
for all things, we are grateful. Amen.

May your church grow strong through what
    we offer,
and may we grow strong through offering it. Amen.

We give what we can to a God who gives us
    everything.
We give what we can to a God who will use it.
We give what we can willingly and gratefully.

Thank you for the good things you give.
Thank you that we can give this back to you. Amen.

All things come from you,
and so we return this money to you. Amen.

We think of the great things we have.
We think of the little we offer you.
We think of you and say thank you. Amen.

We give this to you with grateful hearts.
We give ourselves to you with willing hearts. Amen.

Heads together

Get the congregation to form informal groups of all
ages, get their heads as close as possible to create a
sense of togetherness, and invite them to pray
together. Each person could say a short extempor-
ary prayer if they are willing.

STOP and TeaSPoon

Use either of these tried-and-tested methods to
help prayer times with children and young people:

Using the word STOP, focus on each letter and
what it represents – S for Sorry, T for Thank you, O
for Others and P for Please.

Follow the same pattern with the letters T, S and P
from Teaspoon.

Prayer wall and prayer tree

Cover a wall with some paper and provide marker pens for the congregation to write their prayer needs and answers to prayer as they arrive in church. Another option is a 'prayer tree', with the basic trunk and branches on the wall and leaves available to be written on and stuck to the tree. Use the prayer needs and answers during the prayer time in the service.

All together

Encourage the congregation to speak out the names of people who need prayer all at once. This works well once older people relax into it and children grow in confidence, and could be extended to saying whole prayers individually at the same time.

See the prayer

Put a list of general and specific topics for prayer up on a sheet or projector. Invite everyone in the congregation to say each one out loud, followed by a short time for silent prayer. Then move on to the next subject, and so on.

Directions for prayer

Ask the congregation to stand and face different directions for different prayers. This can be used in many ways:

Turn round and face the back.
(Prayers reflecting on the past, and all that has gone before)

Turn and face the side.
(Prayers thinking about temptations and ways that are wrong)

Turn and face the front.
(Dedication to go forward with God as individuals and as a church)

Thumb prayers

Using the hands in prayer is very important, as much of what we do and express in communication with others and with God is done through our hands:

Hands clenched, thumbs rising.
(Prayers asking God to help us grow with him)

Thumbs moving together.
(Prayers for relationships in families and in the church)

Thumbs down.
(Repentance and confession for wrong things)

Thumbs up.
(Celebrating good things and good times)

Thumbs pointing outwards.
(Prayers for the community outside the church)

Singing prayers

Have you thought about putting prayers to music, or having a response to a popular tune? There are many creative people out there who could make suggestions of music to bring into prayer without it becoming too contrived or complicated.

Prayer ministry

Many churches provide prayer for particular issues, healing, and other needs at the end of services or in a dedicated area during the worship. It is obvious, but so rarely the case, that if you are an intergenerational church this prayer will be open for all ages to access, and that those praying will also represent the different generations in church. Children, young people and adults will need some training and guidance, but there is absolutely no reason why God will not use the prayers of the young as well as the older.

EIGHT

Readings, stories and talks

In an all-age service these three areas – Bible readings, stories and talks – should be so well integrated that it is hard to tell where one ends and another begins. Many of the principles are the same, and therefore they should not be thought of as being distinct from each other.

Bible readings

I was somewhat taken aback a while ago when speaking to a leader at a church I was going to visit. 'We don't usually have a Bible reading in our family services,' he said, with no sense of shame, 'we found it got a bit boring!' I would have hoped that all people involved in leading worship would agree that the Bible is an essential and integral part of any service, and all-age services are certainly no exception. God's word can speak to all ages, and shouldn't be shied away from just because it may take a bit of work to communicate it effectively. Many adults as well as children are no longer reading the Bible as part of their daily routine, and therefore it is becoming even more important to use the Bible for it to be seen as relevant and essential for the Christian life. Before we look at details and suggestions here are a few starter questions:

Is the language and translation appropriate?

Is the chosen passage directly relevant to the theme?

Is it possible to use a story version or dramatised Bible?

Is it well-read, with a sense of life and vitality?

Does it repeat what you are about to act out or tell?

Is there a key phrase or verse which can be focused on?

Translations

There are many English language versions of the Bible, with around 30 easily available. This gives scope for finding and using a translation which is helpful for all the congregation. The use of traditional translations may have its place, and there are many who will argue that certain versions are correct and others are not. But the key to deciding which translation to use during all-age services is whether the language is accessible to children as well as adults, and to unchurched as well as regular attenders. The versions of the Bible I would look at in this context are:

The Good News Bible (Collins / Fontana)

Contemporary English Version (Nelson)

International Children's Bible (Word)

Paraphrased Bibles

There are a large number of children's Bibles on the market which take the more popular stories and paraphrase them. The only warning I would make here is that they go for good narrative, and often miss out the prophecies, poetry, epistles, and more complex accounts of Old Testament battles etc. There are also some excellent paraphrases now available which are designed for use with adults, but are suitable also for all-age services. *The Message* by Eugene Peterson (NavPress) is one excellent example.

Choosing the passage

Make sure that the Bible passage you choose is appropriate for an all-age congregation, and clearly relevant to the theme. Try to avoid reading the whole of a story that is then acted out or presented later in the service, instead read some of it and then dramatise the rest of the story from where the reading ends. Readings should be kept fairly short unless they are presented in a dramatic, visual manner. If necessary, do not be afraid to set the scene before the reading in order to help everyone put it into context. But don't fall into the trap of avoiding more difficult passages and issues because there are children present. We all need to hear the whole of the Bible and learn to apply it to our lives, not just become familiar with the easy and popular stories.

Bringing the words to life

Readings can be tedious if read by one person in the normal 'flat' way which seems to be common in churches. Readers should practise making the passage come alive by varying the voice, changing the tone for different people, using a questioning tone for questions, and so on. This seems natural when reading children bedtime stories, and needs to find its way into our churches. A dynamic delivery of the reading can make the words seem to live and breathe for themselves, and make the meaning much clearer.

Many voices and places

If possible, try having a number of voices in the reading, positioned in different parts of the church. There should be a range of ages, not just children. Make sure that they can hear each other, and that the congregation can hear them too. Try photocopying the passage and dividing it between readers with different colours of highlighter pens or use *The Dramatised Bible*.

Make mistakes

Occasionally it can be fun to read a short passage from the Bible, and then read it again with deliberate mistakes, asking the congregation to wave or stand if they spot a mistake. Not only does this help them listen to it, it also reinforces the meaning.

Visual aids

Think about having pictures on display during the reading, linked with the theme. This section of the service then becomes more attractive to all concerned, and is therefore more likely to be remembered.

Music

Music or a worship song could be played while the reading is given. Make sure that the music used is appropriate, and that it adds to rather than detracts from the reading as a whole. Continuing the music after the reading has ended and inviting the congregation to think about the reading while they listen can be very effective.

Costumes

We will think more about these when we look at storytelling later, but if the passage is about a particular story or character it can help greatly to wear a simple, suitable costume to visually set the scene as you read.

Responsive reading

If you can reproduce the reading for everyone it can help for it to be read antiphonally, either with the leader and congregation or two halves of the congregation taking it in turns to read a verse.

Reading on CD

I once visited a church where a group of young people had recorded the reading, and it was played through the PA system at the appropriate point. This was effective in a number of ways. Firstly the young people delivered it better than they would have if they had been standing in front of the congregation. Secondly the congregation were forced to listen to the words as there was no visual to detract from the message. This wouldn't work every time, but once in a while it can be great.

Split up reading

There is no reason why the reading or readings have to be done at the same point in the service. The reading could be split into two or more parts, read as a continuing story. This works particularly well when each part is introduced with a 'The reading so far . . .' sentence. It may work to have the final part of the reading after the story or talk.

Stories

By this I don't mean what used to be called 'The Children's Address', which confused me immensely as a child, as it never seemed to have anything to do with where I lived! Any story that is communicated in a service should be seen as relevant to all ages, not just the younger end. In many services a story is told at some point after the reading and before the talk. Again it is worth remembering that it can damage the impact if the story is the same as the reading. In all-age services the way stories are told is key to how memorable the whole service and the key learning points are. Telling a story successfully to a mixed-age congregation is not easy, be it a story from the Bible or from your own life. In order to keep the presentation fresh and attractive new, imaginative and challenging ways of telling the story must be considered. But first, think through these questions:

Does the story have a clear point to it?

Is there an interesting or dramatic way it can be told?

Are there sections or verses which it may be better to miss out?

Can it involve the whole congregation, volunteers and visual aids?

Is there a way it can be linked to a real-life situation?

Is it a familiar, jaded passage or challenging, unfamiliar text?

The content and context

When using a story make sure that you know the content and context by heart. Be sure of the reason for using that particular story, and clear on the main emphases (point, character, incident, moral). Take time to consider which parts of the story may confuse, and which language and words may be inappropriate. Most of all make sure that there is a strong beginning and clear end.

Be . . .

Here are a few ways which help in the delivery of stories, making them fresh and active.

. . . seen – visible, prominent, noticeable and mobile.

. . . connected – with, amongst, part of, and moving around.

. . . heard – loud, clear, steady speed, and varied pitch.

. . . confident – build yourself up, practise and avoid nerves.

. . . in control – don't talk over chatter, expect quiet.

. . . communicative – varied eye contact and open body language.

. . . alive – gestures, movement and expressions.

. . . ready – equipment on hand, resources available.

. . . short – keep to time, don't repeat, and focus on the theme.

. . . telling – try not to need to read the story, and tell directly.

. . . sensitive – read the children, moods and watch for body language.

. . . yourself – chat, use your voice, and avoid being patronising.

. . . sure – know your target and how you will get there.

. . . simple – relevant points, plotlines and incidents.

. . . worshipful – not just for fun but for teaching too.

. . . prepared – spiritually as well as practically.

. . . different – variety, unexpected happenings and shock tactics.

Reading the story

This is best avoided, as holding a sheet of paper or putting a book on the lectern can create a barrier between you and the congregation. You may find it better to write the key points of the story on small cards and hold them in your hand to refer to, or write it on a large sheet of paper stuck to a pillar which you can see but the congregation can't!

Drama

There are a number of ways to communicate a story through drama. The key thing is to make sure that the presentation does not detract from the message or plot but enhances it. There are many books, scripts and resources for drama available, and it is therefore not always necessary to produce your own.

To deliver a scripted drama with children takes a great deal of hard work, preparation and practice time. They may be willing to give it a go, but basic questions about how clear the message is and whether the dialogue can be heard must be asked from the outset.

A scripted drama with adults or a mixed-age cast can work very well, especially if some of the people involved are not the ones the congregation would normally expect to be dramatic. But again, be aware that it is a lot of work, and unless it has clarity and a strong impact it is not going to be really effective.

Role play

Role play is a very flexible approach to conveying a story. You can involve some or all of the congregation, play a role yourself, or have 'volunteers' to come out and take part. You may be confident in using varied voice pitches and accents for different characters. The story can be told with a few people chosen at random acting out the roles in the story. They could have simple costumes, hats, large name labels, or other items to differentiate them. As you tell the story move the volunteers around, asking them to say simple lines, or do actions and mimes to fit the story. The whole congregation could play the role of an individual character or a crowd. And be assured that the more you involve people, the more likely it is that you will keep the attention of the whole congregation. Mime can also be an effective and powerful dramatic tool as a performance in itself.

Monologues

It can be very scary to stand and speak completely playing the role of someone else. Some people are able to do this, but others are not. Monologues can be very powerful, especially if trying to encourage the worshippers to look at the story from a different angle. They need to be well written and practised, and not so obscure that it never becomes obvious who the person giving the monologue is pretending to be. Monologues have more dramatic impact if they are not introduced, and if afterwards a few moments are left for thought before the next item.

Visuals and pictures

If you are able to tell a story and use other resources at the same time it can help in getting the theme across. You may have a gifted artist in your church who could do some large pictures to help you illustrate the story, or you may simply want to hold up one item which is relevant to the story as you tell it. Puppets, with or without the skill of ventriloquism, can be great storytellers if used with practice and experience. If you use pictures the usual rules apply: make sure that they are clear and visible, and that there is someone to help you to hold them up at the right time. If you're not confident using visuals and pictures don't do it!

Activities

One way to explore the Bible passage is to get groups of people to do activities together, based on the passage you have chosen. You could get them to do any of the following:

- Draw responses to the passage
- Make objects that relate to the story

- Answer some simple questions
- Discuss the topic and write thoughts on a flipchart sheet
- Prepare a drama of the story
- Choose words that summarise the message

Rhymes, poetry and rap

The way you use words and the words you use are both very important in telling stories. If you use rhymes, especially those which have a response, you are more likely to involve the younger end of the age profile. Poems can be very effective and powerful stories. And raps remain popular, especially if prepared and performed by the young people in the church. Preparation and confidence are again the key elements to using words creatively in these ways.

The following are some but not all of the varied approaches used by successful storytellers. Most have already been mentioned, and many can be combined to provide a really exciting, challenging and attention-grabbing approach:

Read the Bible account of a story, as a simple, gimmick-free approach – this is no bad thing from time to time!

Read from a children's Bible or a paraphrased version when telling more complex or dramatic stories.

Tell the story in your own words after preparation, this is best for cutting out unnecessary or confusing sections.

A rap or poem with plenty of life and rhythm can be especially good if you can get some of the young people involved.

Sing a song that tells the story on its own, without the need for repetition.

Short film clips can communicate very effectively, but check copyright first. Old-fashioned sound-strips can be fun for a change, too.

Playing a DVD with the story on it can help people focus, and provides a vehicle for mimed and improvised drama.

Tell a familiar story with mistakes, asking the congregation to spot the errors and offer you the correct words.

Wearing costumes, even a simple hat or pair of sunglasses, helps inspire the imagination of those watching.

Move around. This is obvious but rarely done! To keep attention move amongst the congregation, even getting them to move for a 'promenade' story too if possible.

Ask the congregation questions. They will listen if they think you are going to pick on them and ask, 'What do you think happens next?' or 'What would you do in that situation?'

Be unpredictable by varying the way you speak, changing the volume, pitch and accent as frequently as possible.

Talk

In so many all-age services this is the bit where it really goes to pot! The songs have been fun, the prayers have been well-prepared, and the visual aids went down a storm. But now the point has come to draw it all together, and you begin to realise with that familiar sinking feeling inside that imperceptibly somewhere along the way the service has gone off-track.

The aim of the talk is to remind the congregation of the messages of the story and reading, and to help them apply those messages to their lives. The talk in an all-age service should be short, simple and relevant to the lives of all of the listeners as well as making sense when put together with the rest of the service. This can seem almost impossible, and it does take work. Think about these questions first:

Is there a clear message that you want all the congregation to understand?

Does it fit in with all that has gone before?

Are there supplementary illustrations relevant to all ages?

Is it in appropriate language?

Does it challenge all listeners to reflect and change?

Connections

The talk is usually used to explain the truths behind the reading and story, and make connections with the realities of day-to-day life. You may want to unpack the story by answering these three questions as the basis for the talk:

1. What was the meaning and message in the context of the time it happened?

2. What do we take from that meaning and message in our world?

3. What does that inspire us to consider, and how should we change as a result?

The key message

There must be one clear point which you want to get across to everyone. It is likely to be fairly simple, but open to development depending on the age of the listener. Some people may think that this is too simplistic and therefore results in shallow teaching, but that doesn't have to be the case. The profound and moving truths about God are essentially simple. The message should have been evident in the other elements of the service, central to your planning, and used as a focal point for prayer as well as learning.

Supplementary messages

There can be room for other thoughts and points to come out of the service in addition to the key point. The supplementary messages should complement the key message, and not in any way cause confusion. Aim for a maximum of three points in total, as after that the younger (and possibly older!) members of the congregation will get confused and forget the key message you are trying to communicate.

Length

Keep the talk relatively short. If you have made full use of the other components of a service then the links will have been obvious, and there will be no need to labour the point. Aim for the combined story and talk to last between 15 and 20 minutes in general, although there is no hard and fast rule. Just remember some of the skills involved in relating to and 'reading' the congregation, and cut your losses if you appear to have lost their concentration.

Talk chunks

As with Bible readings and stories, there is no reason why the talk needs to be given as one whole. It may be more appropriate to split it into two or three chunks, linking it with more story, song or prayer slots. This adds to the variety of the service, while making sure that there is plenty of teaching in there.

Application

The messages you are giving need to be taken further in order to have a lasting effect on the lives of all worshippers, young and old, and applied to aspects of their lives. That will usually mean that it will be necessary to give examples appropriate to different age-groups. For instance, you will need to ask the congregation what it will mean to their lives at home, at school, at work, or with their neighbours.

Ending the talk

Many churches are in the habit of having long sermons, not necessarily because there is plenty to be said, but because that is what always happens! We have all heard preachers using phrases like 'Now for my last point', 'and finally', and 'to conclude', and then we have sat and listened as they went on, and on, and on . . . Once the key message and any other messages have been explained, and you have encouraged the congregation to reflect and change as a result, then your job is done. Do not be afraid to keep the talk short or to stop without too much repetition. It often helps to pray at the end of the talk, repeating the key message and asking God to make it relevant to all of our lives.

Readings, stories and talks

As we have already discovered, these go together closely. Here are twelve suggestions for readings, stories and talks which demonstrate a variety of approaches to putting it all into action. Most of these suggestions will work just as well with different themes and stories.

The Ten Commandments

God gives us guidelines to live by

Reading

Explain that God had a special message for his people, and wanted them to take notice.

Read Exodus 19:16–25, with different voices for Moses and God. Try to ensure that the reader of God's words is not seen.

Story

Explain that the people were on a long journey that would last 40 years, and they didn't really know what they should and shouldn't do. God gave them ten rules to help them do the right thing.

Then teach the 10 Com Rap, with the congregation repeating it line by line. If possible, have each line displayed on a projector or on large individual 'tablets of stone'. Cardboard boxes are good for this.

The 10 Com Rap

(from the book *Ten Commandments*)

He is the only God.
Don't worship the odd.
Be careful what you say.
Have a restful day.
Honour Mum and Dad.
Don't murder or do bad.
Adults – stay together.
Don't steal things ever.
Be honest when you speak.
Have no greed in what you seek.

Talk

Connections: The people were going wrong and needed help. God gave them rules to help them. Those rules have lasted the thousands of years since then, and are still useful for us today. Some of the people ignored God's rules, and some people still do, but that is not the best way to live.

Key message: God gives us guidelines to live by.

Supplementary messages: The rules help us to live well, and not to hurt others. The rules remain the best way to live, even though others ignore them.

Samuel and Eli

Listening to God

Readings

Insert these short readings throughout the service, but before the story:

Everyone must be quick to listen, but slow to speak and slow to become angry.

James 1:19

Hear this, everyone! Listen, all people everywhere.

Psalm 49:1

Wise people listen to advice.

Proverbs 12:15

Do not deceive yourselves by just listening to the word; instead put it into practice.

James 1:22

Speak, your servant is listening.

1 Samuel 3:10

Story

Make two large name labels on string to put around two volunteers' necks, one saying 'Eli' and the other, 'Samuel'. Try to get an adult to play the Eli role. Then tell the story of Samuel and Eli in your own words, based on 1 Samuel 3:1–10. Every time you say either name the congregation should respond:

Samuel: 'He's young, he's young, he's very very young.'

Eli: 'He's old, he's old, he's very very old.'

Talk

Connections: Samuel had to learn to take time out and listen to God. God had a message for him, and he became very important. God wants us to take time too and listen.

Key message: Take time to listen to God

Supplementary messages: We all need to listen to God, however young or old we are. God can use anyone, he can even use you!

Love

God gives us love

Readings

1 Corinthians 13:4–7
This reading should be before the story and talk, with an introduction about how Paul wanted the church in Corinth to understand what love is all about.

Psalm 63:1–5
This second reading should be just before the talk. Introduce by explaining that we should all desire to worship God.

Story

Tell the story of the leper being healed, based on Matthew 8:1–4. Begin by explaining that lepers were not loved by anyone, but feared by all. Yet Jesus was willing to show the man love.

Use a number of volunteers from the congregation to act out the parts to your commentary, and have the worshippers make 'crowd' noises every time you say 'crowd'.

Talk

This talk is in five parts, and you will need various objects to help you. It should be prefaced by the reading from Psalm 63.

1. Is love about romance? (Hold up a red rose.) Love can be about romance but that is only part of the story. This red rose, like romance, may one day die. Love is so much more than this. (Give the red rose to an older person in the congregation.)

2. Is love about presents? (Hold up a wrapped present, perhaps a small box of chocolates.) It is great to get presents, and we all like that. We may even say, 'If you love me you will buy me what I want!' But presents come and go, break or become unwanted. Love is so much more than that. (Give the present away.)

3. Is love about what we want? (Hold up a chocolate bar.) Some people say that they love chocolate, or TV programmes, or fish and chips. But you can't really love those things. We cheapen and weaken what love is really all about if we say things like that. Love is so much more. (Give the chocolate bar away.)

4. Love is about giving. (Hold up four large nails.) Love is about Jesus, who was willing to give everything for us. He was more powerful than romance, presents or the things we want. These nails remind us of the love of Jesus.

Key message: Love is something we should look after, value, treasure, and give. We should want and desire to receive the love that God offers, and be willing to give and share that love with others.

Christingle

Jesus is part of everything

Christingle services occur in many churches and are part of the annual fund-raising programme for the Children's Society.

Reading

Christingle services usually take place around Advent or Christmas, and therefore a Christmas reading is appropriate.

Story and talk

This story and talk is combined, and is in three parts. Each should be based in and told from a different area of the church. You will need the phrase CHRIST IN written up on a large sheet of paper and displayed, and G, L and E on pieces of paper to put with it.

1. Stand near the crib or tree if you have one in place. Ask a child to hold up the letter G. Explain that G is for Gifts. Jesus was a gift which we remember at Christmas, as God sent Jesus as the best present we could ever have. But we all have gifts to use too that come from Jesus. We can share, love, care, etc.

Key message: Christ is a gift from God, and he gives us gifts.

2. Stand near a candle. Ask a child to hold up the letter L. Explain that L is for Light. Jesus brought light to the world. When he had grown up he went from town to town and village to village speaking to people, healing and helping them. He also explained who he was, on one occasion saying 'I am the light of the world'. He brings light to the darkness and sad times in our lives.

Key message: Jesus is the light, and brings light to our dark times.

3. Stand amongst the congregation. Ask a child to hold up the letter E. Explain that E is for Everyone. Because Jesus was the best gift, and because he brings light to all the world, we can all have Jesus with us. Another name for Jesus is Emmanuel, which means 'God is with us'. Jesus wants to be with everyone, including all of us here.

Key message: Jesus wants to be with everyone, but do we want Jesus?

Worry

Trusting God for everything

Readings

If you have access to it read the poem 'The King's Breakfast' by A. A. Milne, from the book *When We Were Very Young*.

Matthew 6:24–34
This Bible reading is best done with someone else holding up a number of objects or drawings at the appropriate points as the passage is read. You will need clothes, food, drink, a bird (inflatable is easy!), birdseed, and flowers.

Story

To make this story more visible dress up as a shepherd with a crook, move among the congregation, and if possible have a live sheep in church (with appropriate floor coverings!).

Charlie the sheep was part of a big family. They spent most of their time happily playing and eating in the fields. One day Charlie was bored and wanted to do some exploring, so he wandered away from the others. He walked a long way across fields, bridges and lanes, through valleys, woods and streams. He was very far from the others when he began to feel hungry, and before long the sky started to get dark. It was then that Charlie realised he had no idea where he had come from or which way he should go to get back to his family. He was lost. As he thought about what to do and ran this way and that he became increasingly worried and frightened, and finally slumped down and cried.

After lying still and weeping for a while it was so dark that Charlie could hardly see anything, and the breeze was rustling in the trees. Then he heard a noise. As he crouched down his heart pounded. Was it a wolf? Could it be a lion? Would he survive? He was really worried now, and so scared that he couldn't even move. Charlie plucked up all his courage and opened his eyes, looking towards the noise. But he didn't see a wolf or a lion. Instead he saw the familiar face of the shepherd coming to take him home.

Later Charlie sat cosy and warm in the arms of the shepherd, listening to the bleating of all his friends.

Talk

Explain that we all worry. Some people worry about things that have happened in the past, while others worry about the future. Charlie the sheep was worried because he was lost. He moved from feeling bored to being brave and adventurous, and then to being scared, worried and lonely. When we worry about the future or feel lost who should we turn to?

How do we get help?

In the story the shepherd went out of his way to help Charlie. There are always people around to help us when we get worried, whether we are at school, at work, at home, or retired.

This is a similar story to one Jesus told, and he called himself the Good Shepherd. Jesus wanted people to know that he is willing to be a shepherd for us, finding us and helping us when we worry or struggle.

Key message: God cares for us, whatever we worry about.

Supplementary messages: When we feel lost we can turn to Jesus. Worry gets in the way of our life.

Remembrance

God is always with us

Readings

The readings should be split and given at separate times, with the appropriate part of the talk after each reading. Explain before the first reading that the psalms were written to praise God, despite the suffering that people often went through. They remind us that God is faithful.

First reading: Psalm 111:1–6

Second reading: Psalm 111:7–10

Story

If possible, use an account from your own family or someone in church who has been affected by the pain and sorrow of war. Try not to make it too sad or harrowing, but be honest about what war causes. There may also be a church link with war zones abroad through missionaries which can be explored.

Alternatively you may want to talk about what happened during the First World War, when millions of soldiers, some very young, died in dreadful conditions. Then move on to the end of the First World War, on 11 November 1918. Hold up a clock. Explain that it reminds us of the past, and eleven o'clock on 11 November 1918. It reminds us that time is passing. It also reminds us that there is a future.

Talk one

God is always with us, whether we realise it or not. God knew the pain of those who have died or been injured in wars and those close to them, and he knows the pain of those here who remember them with sadness. We should also remember what God does for us all the time, not just in the past (verse 4). God reminds us to remember by the happy memories we have in our heads and the life we live.

Key message: God knows the pain that people have been through in the past, some of it caused through war.

Talk two

This psalm talks of God's justice and truth, his everlasting love and his power to set people free

(v.7–9). God can bring peace and freedom to all people so that there really is hope for the future. Our hope for peace starts with us. We have to learn to obey God and live the way he calls us to, forgiving those who upset us and aiming for real peace, not wait for everyone else to do it.

Key message: We all have a part to play in bringing peace to the future.

Ambition

The Tower of Babel

Reading

Philippians 2:1–4
This reading is short, so would lend itself to being read twice, the first time correctly and the second with deliberate mistakes.

Story

Introduce the story by explaining that ambition is wrong if it involves hurting others, being selfish, or thinking we can be as good as God. That's what the people of Babylon thought many thousands of years ago.

This story works well with children and adults involved, and 'bricks' (shoe boxes for instance) to build a wall with. It is a monologue, and a costume would help set the scene.

It was such a shame! All people were living together quite happily and were pleased with the life they led on the plains, hills and valleys. But a few, and it was only a few at first, decided to get clever and that ruined it for all of us.

It all started many years ago, when everyone spoke the same language throughout the world, and people lived in tribes and families all over the place. Then a lot of people headed for the area which we now know as Babylon, because they'd heard that the soil was really rich and crops grew well there. Anyway, soon hundreds of families were there, and more arriving by the day. A few people were putting the straw and soil together with water to make mud bricks which dried in the sun. Then they were building themselves little shelters to live in.

But it was when one or two men wanted to show how great they were that the problems began. 'Let's become famous' they said, deciding that their lives were too unexciting. In the end they planned a tower. It would stand on the plain of Babylon and everyone for miles around would see it. It was an ambitious plan, but they thought they were better than anyone else and could do it. So some bricks were made and the tower began. More bricks were made and the tower got bigger. 'We can build the tower to the clouds and be in charge of everything' they said to each other, thinking of the power they would have and how everyone else would look up to them.

God was saddened by all their work. It was good to be ambitious, but only for the right things. It was good to work hard, but only at the right jobs. 'These people think they can do anything they want!' said God, and he thought of a way he could stop them without causing any harm. 'I will mix up their speech so that they will all talk differently' he decided. 'They will have different languages and not be able to work together without confusion.' And that's what happened.

The first day was quite funny, as people spoke and shouted nonsense to others, and all sorts of mistakes were made. But after a few days some builders got very angry with others, and some families decided to move away with others who spoke the same language. And so people settled all around the world, all speaking in different ways. All because a few men were a little too ambitious.

Talk

Remind the congregation of what the Philippians reading said. It explained that we should do nothing out of ambition for ourselves, and we should treat others properly. Meanwhile the men building the tower at Babel were building out of ambition for themselves, so that they would have power and fame. We should only be ambitious to do what God wants and tell others about him, not to do only what we want. That means at work and at school too, and it is a challenge to all of us.

Key message: Do not be ambitious for yourself.

Supplementary messages: God wants us to do what he wants. Be careful about the way we treat other people.

Doing more

Do everything as well as possible

Readings

These individual verses should be taped with a range of voices, and played at the appropriate point. Then using a flip chart ask the congregation to say what key points the readings make.

. . . when your faith succeeds in facing trials, the result is the ability to endure.

James 1:3

Whoever holds out to the end will be saved.

Matthew 24:13

They are blessed because they have persevered.

James 5:11

. . . let us run with determination the race that lies before us.

Hebrews 12:1

Story

This story has many opportunities to think about what to do. The congregation should be asked each time you come to 'What would you do?' whether to give up, go along with the crowd, or stick in there and do more. Although school-based it is still relevant to the whole congregation.

Miss Snodgrass was the least popular teacher in school. She seemed to shout all the time, and never let anyone get away with doing anything wrong. Everyone dreaded upsetting her. When she was angry she could get really mean and nasty!

During an ordinary lesson one morning the headteacher came in. 'Miss Snodgrass, you must go to the telephone now. There is an urgent message for you. Leave the class, I am sure they will be fine for a couple of minutes.'

What would you do?

As Miss Snodgrass left the room she looked uneasy, and decided to get back there as quickly as she could, just in case. Soon the children heard the last of her footsteps in the corridor.

What would you do?

Then most of them were out of their seats, swapping chairs, shouting and running about. Charlotte and a few others stayed in their places and tried to get on with their work, while one or two stood by the door keeping a lookout for Miss Snodgrass. 'She's coming!' the cry went up . . .

What would you do?

. . . and in a flash they were all sitting appearing to work. In fact Miss Snodgrass wouldn't have thought anything had happened had it not been for the message on the blackboard: 'Miss Snodgrass is a grotbag.'

What would you do?

Her face went through a range of colours including purple, black and yellow. Then she turned to the class in a fury and demanded to know who had written it. No one dared own up, and they were kept in at breaktime.

What would you do?

At lunchtime she tried again, but there was still no explanation. She asked one last time, and Charlotte said she had not done wrong, but she would take the punishment. The class knew that Charlotte could not be to blame as she never did anything wrong.

What would you do?

Miss Snodgrass didn't know what to say, because she knew Charlotte was innocent. In the end she gave Charlotte a punishment of tidying the classroom for a week. Charlotte had taken the punishment on behalf of the whole class.

Talk

Doing more and going further is about everything you do. There are times when you have to try really hard to understand something, or other times when you have to do more to help other people. Doing more, persevering, and not giving up can often be hard and challenging, but once you've done it you feel really good.

Charlotte did more than she needed to by taking the punishment. Nearly all of the children were to blame, but Charlotte went a bit further for the good of them all.

Key message: God expects us to do our best, and go a bit further.

Supplementary messages: Jesus took the blame for us, as Charlotte took the punishment for the class. We have the power of God to help us do more.

Heroes – All Saints

God has a different view of heroes!

Reading

Hebrews 11:23–29

As this is read out have someone hold up a sign saying 'it was faith', and encourage the congregation to join in with the phrase as it appears.

Activity

Prepare a sheet of pictures of heroes from across the generations, and ask the people in small all-age groups to discuss who they are and try to identify them. Make sure you choose people from popular culture, pop music, sport, TV presenting, and so on.

This is easily done by taking pictures from the internet and pasting them onto a word document sheet. After a short while ask for the answers, and while doing so also ask people to say who their heroes are.

Part 1 – Who are heroes?

We often think of famous people, talented people or sports players as heroes, and some of them may be. But God wants us all to be heroes, and we can be if we follow his plan for our lives. We may not become rich or famous, but we will have the satisfaction of knowing that we have done what God made us to do.

Part 2 – Start young

Moses started his life as a hero very young, when his mother placed him in a basket and hid him in order to protect him from death. But a bit later, after he had grown up as a prince in the Pharaoh's family, Moses was still a young man, probably a teenager, when he stood up for what was right. He started young. He saw someone being really badly treated and stepped in, doing the right thing.

Heroes often start young. There's no reason why the young people here can't be heroes at school and college, speaking up for what they believe and defending the Church and God. Many of the older people here are heroes, and they started young! Heroes start young.

Part 3 – Stick at it

Moses left his home after stepping in and causing another man who was doing bad things to die. He worked as a shepherd, and could have stayed there out of the way. But God had a plan for Moses, and he stuck at it. He responded to God when he called him by speaking through a burning bush, and he stuck at it when time and time again Pharaoh refused to let the people that Moses was leading go.

Heroes, whether they start young or not, need to stick at it! It is never easy doing what God wants us to do, and there will always be big challenges and obstacles along the way. God gives us the strength to cope through the Holy Spirit, but it takes real determination to stick at it . . . at home, at work, at school, or wherever we are.

Part 4 – Serve

Moses left a fairly safe life as a shepherd and went to lead God's people from slavery, through dangers, and into the desert. He was called to serve the people, and continued to do it despite the difficult times they went through. Often the people would moan, like the occasion when they were in the desert and were hungry. Moses served them by praying to God and obeying him, and God provided the food they needed. Moses continued to serve the people until he died at a great age.

God needs heroes who start young, who stick at it, and who are willing to serve others, and that's what we as followers should be doing. Heroes put serving others first, and do so because God loves everyone and we should follow that example.

Conclusion

Whoever our heroes are, and whatever they may have done or be able to do, God wants us to be heroes for him. Heroes can start young, heroes have to stick at it, and heroes learn to serve.

God's ABC

Talk with discussion and contributions from the congregation.

This looks at the nature of God, and you will need to be flexible as some of the suggestions you get from the congregation may not match those suggested here.

Readings

These readings give a little indication of what God is like:

Isaiah 43:1–7

Psalm 107:1–3

Psalm 136

Romans 11: 33–36

Split the congregation into all-age groups, and ask them to think of a word about God beginning with each letter of the alphabet. It would save time to allocate five or six letters to each group to think about. After some time to discuss start to get the suggestions, working through the alphabet from A–Z. You may want to split this talk into two or three bits, and do them separately at different points during the service. It will help you to have the alphabet either on sheets of paper or projected.

AMAZING

BRILLIANT

CREATOR

DEITY

EVERLASTING

FORGIVING

GREAT

HOLY

INCREDIBLE

JUST

KIND

LOVING

MAKER

NEEDED

OPEN

PATIENT

QUIET

REAL

SPECIAL

TRUTH

UNBEATABLE

VALUABLE

WONDERFUL

[E]XTRAORDINARY

YOUNG AND OLD

ZILLIAN (beyond number)

Right and wrong

God helps us do what is right

Readings and stories

This is an active story with two readings along the way. It is split into three parts. The readings should be from three different voices of mixed ages.

Explain to the congregation that one end of the church is the beginning and the other is the end. They must point to the correct place every time you say 'beginning' or 'end'. Also they should put their thumbs up for 'right' and down for 'wrong'. Then read this story:

God was there in the beginning, and everything was right. There was no end to the things he made. There was nothing at the beginning, but after a week he had made the world and all the things in it just right. At the end of the week of creation he decided that it had been a good beginning. Very soon two brothers, Cain and Abel, got angry with each other, which was wrong. Cain killed Abel, and the end of the peace came. People were beginning to damage the world that God had made and do wrong. God knew it was right to wash the world but protect people who did right, so he sent a flood. After the end of the flood God sent a sign, saying it was the beginning of a new friendship between God and people.

Reading 1: Genesis 9:8–17

But even after the end of the flood people still ignored God and did wrong. God was beginning to get really fed up with people, so he gave them some clear right and wrong rules. Moses was sent up a hillside and spoke to God. God gave Moses the Ten Commandments, and told the people that they explained what were the right things to do.

Reading 2: Exodus 20:1–17

God thought that the Ten Commandments would mark the end of problems, but again the people were beginning to do wrong. In the end God sent his own son, beginning as a baby born in a stable. Jesus did right all his life, but at the end the people did wrong by hanging him on the cross. He was willing to die for all the wrongs that people do. But that was just the beginning of Christianity, for Jesus came alive again and went up to heaven to be with his and our Father God. The end is still to come, and just like he was there in the beginning, God will be there at the end. If people do right or wrong, God is still there.

Talk

You may want to use your thumbs again as you speak.

There are some things in our world which are right and others which we know are wrong. There are also some things happening in school, home or work which we know are right, and others which we know are wrong. Everything in life could be better if a few of the wrong things became right things. Instead of being unkind, insulting or hurt-ing others we could all try to be kind and helpful. Instead of nagging, being bossy or being selfish we could be patient and think of other people more. These are only small things, but each small thing makes the world just a little better for everyone.

Key message: God helps us work out what is right and wrong.

Supplementary messages: We can make a difference in the world by doing right. God sent his son to die for all of us.

A part to play

Our role in God's plan

Readings

These readings can be given together, but preferably with different voices and from different locations within the church.
Mark 1:14, 15
Luke 9:46–48
Acts 1:6–8
1 Corinthians 12:21–27

Story

This story includes simple words for the disciples to learn and say. You will therefore need a few volunteers to play those parts who have practised beforehand, or who can read the words as they go along.

Jesus was walking along the shore of Lake Galilee. He was a familiar figure there, and the fishermen had got used to seeing him. 'Oh, there's Jesus, the carpenter's son,' they said as they sewed their nets one day. Jesus had been speaking in the local village about how everyone should believe God's good news, and he was the talk of the area. Jesus sat down near the fishermen, the brothers Simon and Andrew, and spoke to them for a while. Then he said to them, 'Come, leave your nets and follow me. I will teach you how to catch men for God, instead of catching fish!' 'We will leave our boats and come with you,' the fishermen said, and they did! After that more fishermen as well as a taxman, a politician and others all left what they were doing, their work and their businesses, and joined Jesus. They were his friends, his disciples.

'I'm better than you', 'No, I'm better than you' said the disciples to each other. 'No, I know that Jesus loves me more', 'You're wrong, I'm his favourite . . .'

and so it went on. The disciples had been with Jesus for many months by this time. They had seen him do amazing miracles and they had listened to his challenging and wise words. They had talked with Jesus, helped him, and even been asked to pray for people to be healed themselves. None of them ever expected this to happen. They knew that he was something very special, and they wanted to be closest to him and loved most by him.

'I don't believe this,' said one disciple, looking up at the cross. 'After all we have been through with Jesus over these three years. Now he is hanging and dying there like any criminal.' Jesus had been arrested, beaten, and finally hung on the cross. The religious leaders wanted him killed because he threatened their power. 'I don't know what we shall do now,' the disciples said to each other, full of sadness and despair. They had no idea what to do next, but God had a plan for them.

'I still can't believe that Jesus is alive again!' said the disciples as they walked across the field together with Jesus. Then he stopped them, and explained that they had still got a job to do. When the Holy Spirit from God came to them they were to continue to spread the message about Jesus. Then, right before their eyes, Jesus vanished! 'What's happened? Where has he gone? What's going on?' the disciples said. Then an angel appeared in front of them and told them that Jesus had gone to heaven. 'Well, I suppose we had better get on and do what Jesus said,' they told each other as they went back home. And they did!

Talk

The disciples were a mixed bunch, very much like the collection of people here today! When Jesus first called them they didn't know what they would end up doing, and they didn't become perfect. They argued about who was best, and they didn't understand all that Jesus told them. But still they had a part to play. When he died and rose again they thought it was all over, but really it was the beginning. They had a part to play after Jesus went to heaven, and were the founders of the Church.

We have a part to play for God too. We may not really understand everything, and we may make mistakes sometimes. We may not know everything about God, or everything that God has got planned for us. But we all still have a part to play.

Key message: We all have a role to play in God's plan.

Supplementary messages: We don't need to be perfect to work for God, there is work to be done by and for all ages.

NINE

Endings and blessings

I wonder if you have ever been to a service that has literally fizzled out? I guess few of us have missed out on the opportunity to look around, trying to decide whether to sit or stand, start talking or remain quiet, leave or stay. As with the beginnings, there are many good reasons why the end of a service needs to be clearly defined and strong. Before going further into this ask yourself the following questions:

Are the endings clear, and does everyone know what to do?

Does the ending reinforce the theme of the service?

Do the congregation have a clear message in their minds as they leave?

Have you told the congregation about after-service refreshments, etc.?

Singing

If there is a song at the end it should be something which fits with the theme and sends the congregation out with as much buzz and enthusiasm as possible. Ending the service with a traditional hymn is often the way it is done, but does not always help the congregation leave on a high. If you must have a traditional hymn at the end, add another short song done earlier in the service after the hymn, perhaps as a processional or after the blessing. This should keep everyone happy.

Processions

All churches follow slightly different patterns. Some churches have a procession of those involved in the service during the final hymn and before the blessing, which is given from the back of the church. Others have a hymn followed by a blessing or final prayer from the front, and then those involved in leading the service walk to the back to some music. Yet more churches have a final prayer and the leader sits and prays before walking casually to the back. There are no right or wrong ways of doing this, but whatever you do, the congregation must be clear on what is required of them, when they are free to move, and what you will be doing.

Give-aways

If you will be giving things away as a reminder of the theme (see chapter ten) this is best done either at the door as people leave, or while people are in their seats after the final prayer or blessing. For this to be meaningful as much needs to be made of it as possible.

Procession

A good way to end an interactive service is to have a procession that each line of people joins in with, and leads to the refreshments area so people can get themselves a drink. This can be enhanced by music, clapping and even dancing!

Refreshments and fellowship

The informality of an all-age service lends itself to a time after the service for the congregation to gather and enjoy time together. It may be difficult to serve drinks in a church with no kitchen or refreshment facilities, but flasks and orange juice do just as well. Be careful when serving drinks to children in case they have an allergy or hyperactive reaction to sweeteners and colourings, and biscuits should not contain nuts.

Activities after the service

Children and young people often find it hard to remain well-behaved and attentive during a service, although, as we have discovered before, the more interest and variety that is included in the planning of the service the more attentive the children will be. At the end of the service you may want to consider organising games or activities for a few minutes in the church hall or on land outside and give them space to let their hair down and let off steam. Obviously, this should be done with adequate supervision. This gives the children a good time and allows the adults to relax a little more.

Final prayers

There are many set prayers available in service books and outlines to say at the end of the service. You may want to write your own prayer to fit in with the theme of the service, trying to include the key point and supplementary points of the talk. The prayer should lead the congregation to think through the issues involved at their own level.

Ending prayers

Though we are young, though we are old,
though we fail, though we go wrong,
be with us Lord, today and for ever.
Amen.

Now to him, who by his power working in us
is able to do more than we can imagine,
to him, who by his power working in us
is able to do more than we can ask for.
To God be the glory, in the Church and in Jesus,
now and for all time.
Amen.
(Ephesians 3:20, 21)

The service is ending,
new life is beginning,
God's word has been given,
God's word has been learned,
God calls us to work,
we will work for him.
Amen.

May our minds be full of your voice,
our hearts full of your love,
and our thoughts full of your grace.
Amen.

As we go from here help us to take you with us.
Be with us at home, at school, at work.
Speak to us in the noise and in the quiet.
Walk with us on our journey through life.
Amen.

Father God,
be with us as we go from here,
and keep us close to you.
Amen.

Father God,
thank you for your challenge today –
may it last a lifetime.
Amen.

Jesus, you are changing me.
Jesus, you are changing me.
Please change my heart, my mind and my life.
Please change my heart, my mind and my life.
Amen.

We are called to be salt, sharing the flavour
    of Christ.
We are called to be light, shining the light
    of Christ.
We are called – let us answer.
Amen.

God around us,
thank you for this church and this family.
Thank you for our enjoyment and our learning.
Thank you for today.
Amen.

Dear God,
help us to take your message
to the world outside,
and to live it in our lives.
Amen.

Father God,
help me love your message
and live your message.
Amen.

Dear God,
thank you for being with us today.
Thank you for teaching us today.
Thank you for loving us today … and every day.
Amen.

Blessings

Again, many formal blessings can be found in service and prayer books. Some of these are seasonal and therefore based on particular themes, while others are more formal.

Go in peace.
Go with God.
Amen.

May God go with us.
May God go with us.
As we go into the world.
As we go into the world.
Amen.

To the only God, who alone is wise,
be glory through Jesus for ever!
Amen.

May God the Father, Jesus the Saviour,
and the Spirit of creation be with us ever more.
Amen.

The blessing of the Creator God,
the Loving Son, and the Powerful Spirit
be with every one of us for ever.
Amen.

May God the Father, Jesus the Son, and the
    Holy Spirit
go with you from here.
Amen.

(Said to each other)
Go with God, go with Jesus, go with the Spirit.

In the name of the Father, Son and Spirit
go and live for God.
Amen.

The Father, whose gift is love,
the Son, whose gift is life,
and the Spirit, whose gift is energy,
be with us as we love and live for God.
Amen.

Be with us, Father of all,
be with us.
Live in us, Son of life,
live in us.
Move in us, Spirit of heaven,
move in us.
Amen.

Go and live it out
with God the three in one.
Amen.

May the Father go with us
in the world.
May the Son live in us
in the world.
May the Spirit work in us
in the world.
Amen.

God, go with us into the worries of the world.
God, go with us into the desires of the day.
God, go with us into the challenges of
    our community.
God, go with us.

May the Father who made you bless you,
may the Son who saved you bless you,
and may the Spirit who called you bless you.
Amen.

TEN

Give-aways

What do you want the people who attend your all-age service to leave with? There are a number of things which should be with children and adults as the service ends. Hopefully they will leave with a clear understanding of the theme and key message which will have been present in the singing, prayers, teaching and talk. You may also want everyone to leave with a sense of enjoyment and fun, having had a good time in worship. You should also be aiming for some of the congregation to leave with a sense of a work unfinished; that God has still got something to do with them. To help ground all of these things give-aways are ideal in acting as a continuing reminder of God's work in their lives.

What are give-aways?

Give-aways are small items which are given to every member of the worshipping congregation at the end of the service. The give-aways should have a clear link with the theme, and be small and reasonably economical to buy. There are many possibilities, and as you plan the theme of the service it may become obvious whether there is a suitable give-away, and what that may be.

When should give-aways be used?

Give-aways could be seen as a novelty as well as an aide-memoire for the congregation. Like many of the other suggestions in this book, if they are over-used and repeated too often they lose their potency and meaning. To squeeze a give-away to fit a theme falsely makes it pointless, and damages the power of those that do fit well.

Give-away themes

There are many items and objects which fit themes well, others which you will think of as you plan. Here are 24 suggestions, enough to last for many years if give-aways are not too over-used.

1. Jigsaw piece
    A simple jigsaw piece is an inexpensive item to give away. Many people have jigsaws around which have pieces missing, and the whole picture is neither important or desirable. The point is that each of us has a part to play, although often we will not see what the overall picture of life is.

    Themes:
    We all have a part to play.
    God's big plan.

2. Pencil sharpener
    Pencil sharpeners are relatively cheap, and can be bought in bulk from educational suppliers and stationers. They are useful, and therefore will be handled by those who are given one, hopefully reminding people of the theme and key message. Sharpeners make things sharper and more effective, as God wants us to be.

    Themes:
    Sharpening our work for God.
    Sharpened lifestyles.

3. Night light
    Night lights or tea lights are small, easy to get hold of, and cheap, especially from a certain Swedish furniture store! Giving one away to each member of the congregation reminds them of the light of Christ going with them from church and with them into their normal lives. Alternatives could include full-sized candles and mini light bulbs.

    Themes:
    The light of Christ.
    Light in darkness.

4. Pebbles
    This works well if you can persuade the congregation to bring a pebble or small stone with

them to the service, although it is wise to have some ready just in case. Pebbles are very easy to find and meaningful if used in the right way, reminding us that we are all different and have been through varied experiences to make us like we are.

Themes:
  We are all different.
  Giving to God (build an altar with pebbles).

5. Pine cones
It can be quite enjoyable collecting pine cones for the service! They are easily available most of the year on the forest floor in most areas. Pine cones are unchanging, natural and linked with the seasons.

Themes:
  The unchanging nature of God.
  The seasons.

6. Pieces of map
Map writing-paper and old maps will do for this give-away, and both are relatively easy to come by. Cut up the map into squares of about 5cm, and give the small pieces away as a sign of God being with us wherever we are. It can be fun to have a map of the local area so that people are given names they recognise, but that is not vital. Maps remind us of places.

Themes:
  God goes with us.
  We are all part of a bigger map.
  God all over the world.

7. String
Use string or lengths of wool up to 20cm long for this. Small lengths of string are not much use on their own, but if tied together they go a long way and are more useful. String can also represent the ropes that bound Jesus while he was being questioned and beaten.

Themes:
  Tied together and working together.
  The suffering of Jesus.

8. Polo mint
Polo mints are famous for the hole in the middle and the mint around the outside. This can remind us of the never-ending love of God, which goes on continuously, or the hole inside us all which

needs the love of God to fill it in. Polo mints will not last long once they are given out, but the image should stay a lot longer!

Themes:
  The never-ending love of God.
  The hole inside of us which needs God to fill.

9. Mirror
It is safer to get hold of mirror card, available from scrap stores and craft suppliers. The mirror reminds us of our own nature – what we look like, and what we see in the mirror. God sees beyond the appearance, and knows what is going on inside us all, yet he still loves us.

Themes:
  God knows us well.
  We are all created in the image of God.

10. Lego
Lego, Duplo and other such products are not cheap, but many homes have boxes of the stuff long-since banished to the loft never to be seen again! One piece of Lego is not much use on its own, and can do little. Together it is much more powerful and worthwhile. That's how God wants us to be.

Themes:
  Building God's kingdom.
  Working together for God.

11. Plasticine
Plasticine, Fimo or modelling clay are all suitable and relatively inexpensive. The key to plasticine is that it can be modelled into whatever shape we want. God desires to mould us and make us more like him.

Themes:
  Being moulded by God.
  Becoming more like God.

12. Eraser
Small pencil erasers are very cheap, especially if bought in bulk from educational suppliers or stationers. Most children will have them, many will collect them! Erasers are used to rub out and remove evidence of mistakes, making it possible to start afresh and do a better job the next time around.

Themes:

God removes our sins.

Making a fresh start.

13. Feather

Small feathers can be bought or found and collected, although remember that you will need one for every member of the congregation. Feathers remind us of the passage in Matthew 6:24–34 which tells us that the birds do not worry about what to wear because God provides all they need.

Themes:

God creates and provides.

Do not worry.

14. Rock salt

Rock salt is relatively easily available in supermarkets and specialist shops. Salt adds flavour as well as historically being used to preserve food. Jesus asks all of us who believe in him to be salt in the world, bringing the flavour of Jesus to everyone we see and meet. Being salt in the world is more about how we live than what we say.

Themes:

Bringing the flavour of Jesus to the world.

Being different.

15. Bell

For this you will need a large number of small bells used in baby rattles and soft toys. They are available from old-fashioned haberdashery stores and craft stores. Bells ring to remind us of things. They can remind us that we should keep clear, as in the gospel accounts of Jesus healing lepers. They also remind us to get ready, for instance church bells ring to call us to worship.

Themes:

Get ready for Jesus at Advent.

Jesus heals the unclean.

16. Calendar

Old calendars or small calendar books are easy to get hold of, and do not need to relate to actual dates. Calendars tell us the date, and indicate all that has happened in the past and the future. They mark the passing of time and give us space to think about what is going to happen next.

Themes:

God in the past, healing our guilt and memories.

God with us in the future.

17. Coin

The value of the coin is not as important as the message. You may be able to persuade a bank to give you new, shiny coins which look good. Make sure that each coin is the same. Coins have value, and although on their own they may not appear to be much, together they can be powerful.

Themes:

God values us all equally.

We are all of value to God.

We are more powerful together than on our own.

18. Nail

Giving a nail is a familiar reminder of the suffering and death of Jesus. The nails should be blunt, and it may be necessary to file down the point if they are sharp. Long nails provide more effective imagery.

Themes:

The suffering and death of Jesus.

Love.

19. Seeds

Seeds are easily available. The cheapest and most effective are sunflower seeds, available from garden centres and pet food shops. Seeds grow into something bigger and better, but they have to be planted in good soil first to begin growing. We all have the seed of God's love inside us, but we must let it grow.

Themes:

Growing in God's love.

God's kingdom grows from us, the seeds.

20. Smile sticker

Smile stickers are widely available in shops and from educational suppliers, and the more you buy the cheaper they are. A smile reminds us of happiness, perhaps the happiness of a healed leper from the gospels of our happiness when we know that Jesus loves us, and will love us forever.

Themes:

The happiness that God gives.

Happiness of individuals (healings, God's people, etc.).

21. Magnet

Small magnets are easily available. A magnet reminds us that there are many things that can pull us away from God, but we know that God is always there and we can return to him.

Themes:
Going God's way in life.
Temptation.

22. Foam hands

Small foam hands can be bought from educational suppliers and other outlets, and have many uses. As a give-away a foam hand reminds us of the love of God who takes us by the hand and leads us.

Themes:
Safety in God's hands.
Hands to serve.

23. Pipe cleaner

Pipe cleaners are still a great resource, and can be shaped easily. Many children will find that they concentrate better if fiddling with one, too! A pipe cleaner can show that God makes us and changes us – we are all part of his creation.

Themes:
Created by God.
We can change as God works with us.

24. Love hearts

These sweets can be bought in mini-tubes, and are becoming increasingly popular at weddings. The love hearts are a reminder of God's love for us, and the fact that whatever we do God's love doesn't change.

Themes:
God loves us whatever!
Loving others.

This is not an exhaustive list of small items to give away at the end of a service, but they give an idea of what can be done. Give-aways do help the congregation take more than memories away from the service, giving them a focal point for continued thinking and worship.

ELEVEN

Living dangerously

How many times have you heard, 'Oh, we tried that in 1947 and we're not going to try it again,' said in your church? Tradition lives and reigns in church, but there is a need to modernise and do things differently if churches are to reach out to new generations in a culturally relevant way. They need to live dangerously!

Breaking the mould

There are plenty of moulds in every church that need breaking. They may be based around tradition, a lack of challenge, fear, or even that things were tried in the past. There are many reasons why people do not want to do challenging things. They may be scared of what could happen, fearing that to do more modern services or to reach out effectively to the community could change the whole nature of the church, and they don't want it to change. Some base their thinking on tales of what others have reported from other churches. There may be a touch of jealousy towards the people who are trying to change things, coming out with classic phrases like, 'They've only been in the church five minutes and now they want it all their own way,' and 'They can't do services – they're not licensed / accredited / recognised / on note / official.' Sadly there are still many churches that simply don't want young people around, but the cost of this is high. Churches that feel and demonstrate a lack of vision in these ways are limiting the life of the Church.

Hope for the future

However, it is not all bad news. Increasingly churches are willing to do a few things radically different, and approach familiar services in an unfamiliar way. All-age is beginning to mean just that, not a service where there is the briefest of nods towards children and young people, but a service where they are integral to it. The voices of children rather than those who used to be children are being heard, and even listened to.

Living dangerously

These ideas and suggestions will not work in every church and are not appropriate to every situation. Some are radical, and will take some working on to make them fit any given situation. Some have elements that could be tried, while doing the whole thing would be too much. Most of all they challenge the thinking behind and the delivery of all-age worship, and are worth considering.

1. Asking all ages
    Produce a questionnaire for all ages about what they would like to see in all-age services. For younger children this should be done in small groups, with an adult leading the discussion but an older child reporting back. Adults could do their questionnaires after or during discussions in cell groups or home groups. The church must be willing to seriously consider all suggestions, and put as many as possible into action. Remember that if people see a little of what they suggest in a service they are more likely to feel that they are part of it, however young or old they are.

2. Look around
    Have a look around at other churches in your area that seem to do all-age worship well. Ask them for their advice, and invite them to your church to conduct an all-age service from time to time. Also don't be afraid to seek help from other people with reputations for good training and advice in your area, perhaps who work for other agencies such as CPAS or Scripture Union, or who work for your denomination. There is nothing wrong with asking for help from outside the church, although this in itself can damage the pride of your own church leaders as well as swelling the pride of those you consult, so do handle it with care and tact!

3. Teams that work

   Develop a team of people all of whom have varied gifts and abilities. The team should include people of all ages, including children and teenagers. Use them as a 'pool', with each one taking part with others in the planning and leading of an all-age service on a rota basis. Those who plan the service do not necessarily need to be the ones involved in the delivery or leading of it. The issue of who is involved in leading the service is an important one in many churches, and has to be worked out on an individual basis. The people in the church who may be licensed or approved may not be the ones who are gifted to be involved in all-age worship. On the other hand, all-age worship should never be seen as a service in which to allow someone to practise leading worship or to test them, as that devalues both their gifts and the whole service. Having a range of people involved ensures fresh ideas each time and stops one individual being landed with all the all-age services and therefore becoming stale. Most of all it lives out in reality what church working together should be all about.

4. Sitting and standing

   We have already looked at actions and movements in relation to all-age worship. Try reversing things from time to time by standing for prayers and sitting for singing. Remember to point out that if someone very important walked into a room we would probably stand to greet them, so there is nothing wrong with standing to pray or to learn in the presence of God. This has a purpose in bringing variety and a sense of the unexpected into the worship, as both sitting and standing are acceptable in God's sight.

5. All-age all the time

   Some churches are now making every Sunday morning service a service for all ages. If this is done they should be genuine all-age services, not adult services with the children given colouring sheets or other meaningless things to do to occupy them. To do good-quality all-age services every week is very challenging, but possible if suitable commitment and resources are given. But it is difficult to ensure enough variety and energy if these services occur too often. Special services could also be considered as good cases for the all-age treatment. Children should be welcomed to baptisms, confirmations, inductions, commissionings, civic services and all other services, and those services should take into account that the church is about all the people, not just the older ones. This may mean that some of the more formal services will need to be radically re-thought, which is not such a bad thing in most cases!

6. All-age midweek

   The all-age service is for many churches the best attended, and yet there are still families and young people who cannot worship on Sundays due to family and work commitments. A short all-age service in the middle of the week, perhaps after school or early in the evening, can help in establishing the value of families working together, and allow worship to take place without the Sunday morning time pressures that are often felt. This could take place in a more neutral venue such as the local school or the church hall, and as it is not part of the formal Sunday set-up more flexibility about those who lead it is possible.

7. Children in charge

   Many children are confident and competent in leadership, yet the church expects them to be quiet and subservient until they reach a certain age. There is a clear need for all-age services to be led by people of all ages, not just wheeling on children to do a short reading, sing a childish song, or collect up the offering. Children should be seen to be part of the worship by introducing items, leading worship, and giving talks. Inevitably this will mean a great deal of work by planning teams and other adults, but it is worth it for the clear point it makes. Who better to communicate to a child or teenager in your church than one of their peers?

8. Adults out!

   In most churches the children leave the main service and go to their own groups at some stage during the service on the majority of Sundays. This is often preceded by a short and not always appropriate 'children's talk'. If it is time for the younger people in your church to get their own back try doing things the other way. Have a Children and Young People service occasionally, including a very short talk for adults near the start. Then the adults should leave and go to groups in the rooms usually reserved for the children's activities. If in your church they are the least attractive rooms such as damp church halls and smelly store rooms the adults may learn something about how they value their children in the process!

9. All-age in the community

    Where are the people in your community on a Sunday morning? Many will be at the local supermarket, garden centre or park. Some churches and denominations are already taking up the challenge to provide short all-age services in town centres, retail parks and supermarkets. You may be in an area where parks, caravan parks and beaches are popular on Sundays, especially in the warmer months of the year, and the last thing people want to do is give up an hour or two sitting in a dull church in formal clothes. If you take your all-age service to your community you will need to think it through carefully to make sure it is completely 'cringe-free' and appropriate to someone who may only catch a few minutes. Some people will stop and listen while others will walk past, but if nothing else it says to them that their local church is willing to be out there with the people it is trying to serve. A large number of the population have fears and doubts about going in to church, so why not take the church to them?

10. Evening all-age

    As well as the day and location of all-age services, it is worth considering the time that they are held too. An early service, say 9.30am or earlier, may be good for families that want to get up and go and have a lot planned for the day, but very difficult to draw families with very young children or teenagers to. All-age services in mornings or afternoons naturally exclude any children from the family of the church who spend most or even some weekends with their other non-resident parent. In addition, there are so many attractions on a Sunday that it is hard for any family to be totally committed to church during the day. Early evening all-age services may be a way to address some of these problems as long as they end in time for children to go home to bed ready for the week ahead, thinking as they do of God and the worship they have just enjoyed.

TWELVE

Resources

This is a short list of publishers and resources that I am aware of and have used though of course you may be aware of others.

Music and songs

Songs of Fellowship for Kids
This is a collection of fairly recent songs which includes some older classics too. Many of the songs would be new to most churches, and it offers a range of lively and quiet songs.

Spring Harvest Kids Praise Party
ICC produce all the music connected with large Christian events such as Spring Harvest and the Keswick Convention. There is a new compilation, *The Big Book of Spring Harvest Kids Praise*, which contains many children's songs, and each year a new *Kids Praise Party* book is released, along with *Kids Praise Party* and *Pre-School Praise* CDs and backing tracks. These feature the best of new worship songs written specifically for children.

Junior Praise
The *Junior Praise* series is now a little out of date but is still widely used in many churches. Some of the songs have value, but others are definitely a little brown around the edges!

Kidsource and Kidsource 2
Kevin Mayhew Ltd produces *Kidsource* and *Kidsource* 2. They are collections of songs for children and have been compiled by Alan Price, a well-respected children's worship leader. This is the largest selection of songs currently available and draws from a range of styles and backgrounds, making it an ideal book for everyone who wants a range to choose from as they lead children in worship.

Out of the Ark Music
Out of the Ark work principally in producing catchy and appropriate songs for school worship, with backing tracks and music resources. Some churches are finding that their songs work well, particularly for special and seasonal occasions.

Bibles

Good News Bible

International Children's Bible

New International Version

Contemporary English Version

The Message

The Lion Children's Bible

The Dramatised Bible

Schemes and magazines for children's work with ideas for all-age services

Scripture Press

Scripture Union Light materials and www.lightlive.co.uk (SU)

Roots (Roots)

Holiday Club outlines (SU/BRF)

Other books and resources for all-age worship

Top Tips for All-Age Worship (SU)
Worship Words (Kevin Mayhew Ltd)

There are simply too many other books to list here! Books about all-age worship, drama scripts, and prayers for children are produced by Scripture Union, Kevin Mayhew Ltd, Lion, BRF and other publishers. The best approach would be to go and have a look on the shelves of your local Christian bookshop or do some web searching of publishers' websites.

You will also enjoy:

All Together Worship
1501162

The Storyteller
1501164

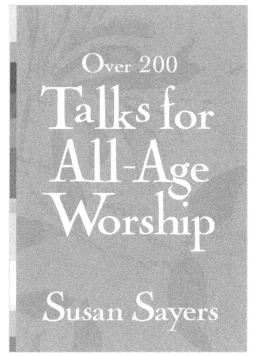

Over 200 Talks for All-Age Worship
1501177

The Feast is Ready to Begin
1501186

CPSIA information can be obtained
at www.ICGtesting.com
Printed in the USA
BVHW010713200520
579993BV00021B/60